The Given and the Made

The Given and the Made,

Strategies of Poetic Redefinition

Helen Vendler

HARVARD UNIVERSITY PRESS
Cambridge, Massachusetts
1995

Library of Congress Cataloging-in-Publication Data

Vendler, Helen Hennessy.
  The given and the made : strategies of poetic redefinition / Helen Vendler.
    p.   cm.
  Originally presented as the author's T. S. Eliot memorial lectures
(Canterbury, University of Kent).
  ISBN 0-674-35431-1 (cloth)
  ISBN 0-674-35432-X (pbk.)
  1. American poetry—20th century—History and criticism—Theory, etc.
2. Berryman, John, 1914–1972—Criticism and interpretation.   3. Lowell,
Robert, 1917–1977—Criticism and interpretation.   4. Graham, Jorie—
Criticism and interpretation.   5. Dove, Rita—Criticism and interpretation.
6. Self in literature.   I. Title.
PS323.5.V39   1995
810.9'005—dc20   95-6765
                                                                                    CIP

Contents

Acknowledgements

The T.S. Eliot Memorial Lectures (1993) at the University of Kent were the occasion for my writing this book. I am very grateful to Mr Christopher Cherry, Master of Eliot College, for his kind hospitality during my stay. Thanks are also due to Faber and Faber.

Those named below have graciously given me permission to reprint as follows: Farrar, Straus, & Giroux for the poetry of John Berryman and Robert Lowell; The Ecco Press for the poetry of Jorie Graham; Rita Dove for her poetry; The University Library of the University of Minnesota and Mrs John Berryman (Kate Donahue) for unpublished writings of John Berryman. I am indebted to Susan Welby for help in manuscript preparation.

Introduction

This book began as the T. S. Eliot Memorial Lectures delivered at the University of Kent at Canterbury. No twentieth-century poet more deserves commemoration than Eliot, a poet who gave us a new, painful, and haunting music, setting poetry on altogether unforeseen paths. I saw T. S. Eliot only once, in 1950, when I heard him deliver a memorial lecture at Harvard in honor of Theodore Spencer, repeating, though in prose, the elegiac gesture of poets:

> So may some gentle Muse
> With lucky words favour my destined urn,
> And as he passes turn,
> And bid fair peace to my sable shroud.

The chain of public literary commemoration is forged of the golden links of elegy and the silver links of memorial lectures. But the most moving commemorations are perhaps the private ones of friendship: Robert Lowell, when Eliot died, acknowledged his own debt to the poet in a letter to Valerie Eliot:

There was no one else who could both write and tell us how to write. . . . There was no doubt of the greatness. . . . No older man so touched something personal in my depths.[1]

And in due course Eliot became one of Lowell's snapshots in

the volume *History*: 'Ah Tom, one muse, one music' wrote Lowell as his words of fair peace.[2]

Eliot requires no commemoration to ensure his literary immortality; his poems alone give him that. But, as Shakespeare in Sonnet 101 says to his reluctant Muse, who protests that the visible worth of the young man makes commendation redundant,

> Because he needs no praise, wilt thou be dumb?
> Excuse not silence so . . .

I hope here to commemorate Eliot, who needs no praise, by looking at the achievement of some of his heirs, for all of whom he made 'American poet' a title of pride.

Before coming to my special topic – what a poet makes of an unasked-for *donnée* – let me say a word about the genre I am treating. I will be considering, through four examples, some possibilities for lyric in America after the second World War; that is, how the inner life of that time – our time – can be accurately and compellingly represented in brief verbal patterns. Lyric is still pre-eminently the non-social genre: though normative narrative and normative drama require at least two characters and are therefore ineluctably social, normative lyric requires not a character but a voice, one engaged in solitary meditation. Meditation may of course include direct address, so much so that some theorists have called apostrophe the defining trope of lyric; but the person addressed is, in the normative lyric, always silent and almost always absent. Only one consciousness, and that an abstract one, is present in the normative lyric.

The relation of the reader to the speaker of the normative lyric is one that has been variously described. Both John Stuart Mill and T. S. Eliot, for instance, thought that the reader 'overhears' the speaker of the lyric, as the audience overhears the soliloquies of Hamlet. Others, like Jon Stallworthy, have preferred, as I do myself, to see the reader as the true speaker of the lyric. In this view, the lyric is a script written for performance by the reader – who, as soon as he enters the lyric, is no longer a reader but rather an utterer, saying the words of the poem *in propria persona*, internally and with proprietary feeling. For poems that are overheard, I prefer to keep the name 'dramatic monologue'; in such a poem the reader is genuinely placed in the position of overhearing someone else, clearly not himself, speak aloud to yet another person. I reserve the name 'lyric' for poems that make their reader their solitary speaker.

No single description fits all lyrics, but I will proceed on the assumption that the purpose of lyric, as a genre, is to represent an inner life in such a manner that it is assumable by others. The inner life of anyone may of course have many aims and thoughts directed to social purposes; but the inner life is by definition one not engaged directly *in* social life. Rather, it is engaged in a reflective look at its own processes of thought and feeling. Of course it may, in that moment, urge social action on itself. But social transactions as such cannot take place in lyric as they do in narrative or drama.

Because the inner life is partly constructed through legitimating vehicles (myths, social positions, religious dogma, ritual practice, gender roles) which undergo historical and cultural change, paying attention to poetic strategies necessarily entails awareness of the existential possibilities available at a given historical moment. In choosing to look at representations of the inner life – itself nowadays an increasingly problematic notion – through four American poets, I have confined myself to two generations: the postwar generation represented by Robert Lowell and John Berryman, and the present generation represented by Rita Dove and Jorie Graham. These choices are relatively arbitrary, but they have the advantage of displaying rather little overlap in the themes of the poets.

I have wanted, with respect to the thematic material of each poet, to discuss some personal *donnée* which the poet could not avoid treating, and to see how he or she found symbolic equivalents for it, and developed that material imaginatively over time. Lowell's primary phantasmagoria is history; Berryman's the Freudian myth of the Id; Dove's, the imagination of forms of blackness; and Graham's, the realm of the virtual or invisible and its relation to the material world. These are developments from inescapable existential *données*: Lowell's genealogy gave him history; Berryman's uncontrollable manic-depressive illness and severe alcoholism gave him the disgraceful Id; Dove's skin-color gave her blackness. In Graham's case, her trilingual education gave her a sense of multiple linguistic, and therefore virtual, realms to square against material life.

These poets bring with them an interesting heap of inner burdens and advantages; and they are poets good enough not to give up on the vexations of complex representation. The gender divide between generations as I take them up here is in itself unimportant, but perhaps of historical interest, given the recent flourishing of American women poets after the relatively solitary eminence, in their respective moments, of Dickinson, Moore, Plath, and Bishop. I want to trace, for each of my four poets, the literary and imaginative problems that arise as he or she attempts to represent an inescapable *donnée*, and to emphasize the structural and symbolic aesthetic strategies to which each has been driven in coping with those problems over time, and making, out of the problematic, the aesthetic.

I
ROBERT LOWELL
AND HISTORY

'History was his eye-opener and his nightcap.'[1]

The wonderfully tense relation between history and lyric was certainly not new when Lowell encountered it: his models Milton and Wordsworth, in their political sonnets, had faced it and outfaced it. Yet lyric history was not the central problem for either Milton or Wordsworth, since their ultimate interest lay in the narrative continuity proper to epic rather than in the glimpse proper to lyric. In epic, their genius had room to expand historical narrative – whether Biblical or personal – into the form its crowdedness would seem to require. The problem of history was more acute for Whitman, who remained a lyric poet all his life, yet whose ambitions were also epic. In an 1860 poem now called 'Thoughts–6: "Of What I Write"' Whitman declares that histories, 'however complete', are 'less complete' than what he writes from himself, which he names 'the resumé.'[2] For Whitman, as later for Mallarmé, the world exists in order to end up in a book; and the book is one written by a single lyric poet. The actions we call history, and their written chronicles which we also confusingly call history, need to be converted into what Whitman in 1876 Platonically named 'eidólons.' These are images, images already invested with compelling form, that form which can be conferred only by the imaginative mind:

[3]

Ever the mutable,

Ever materials, changing, crumbling, re-cohering,
Ever the ateliers, the factories divine,
Issuing eidólons.[3]

The ways in which Whitman folded epic images into lyric, history into feeling, are themselves worth a study. Lowell continues and reworks these strategies in his public political poems, but he had to find new means to record private history. Lowell's youthful idea of history, which was a public one stemming from the participation of so many of his ancestors in public history, was gleaned at first from his omnivorous and compulsive reading of chronicles, from the Bible and Homer to biographies of French and American political and military heroes. He then began to convert his reading into verse: we hear of him at his preparatory school planning a long work in Spenserian stanzas called 'Jonah' (echoes of which survive in 'The Quaker Graveyard in Nantucket'), and later, going to call on Robert Frost 'with a huge epic on the First Crusade, all written out in clumsy longhand on lined paper.'[4] At Baton Rouge, he envisions a long blank verse 'hell and damnation poem against England,'[5] taking, we may suppose, a fiercely political stand. Yet, when Lowell reminisced later about the connection between poetry and events, he refused *engagé* poetry, saying of his generation:

We believed in form, that *that* was very important. . . . We would say that the ideal poet is Shakespeare, who is not a poet of ideology but a poet of experience and tragedy.[6]

Lowell could dispense with ideology, but never with history: as Randall Jarrell's prescient review of *Land of Unlikeness* says of Lowell, 'His harshest propositions flower out of facts.'[7] Lowell could not escape historical facts – he was bursting with them all his life – but he needed to decide which facts mattered. Lowell spent his whole career defining public and private forms of poetic history made out of different sorts of 'poor passing facts' – facts which are not, it is important to say, taken singly, but constellated in fixed relations (different at each of his phases) to each other.

In Lowell's rebellious first idea of history, the lens of the converted present determines the description of the blighted political past; and no contemporary poet could be more 'politically correct' than the young Lowell standing at the cenotaph of his Winslow ancestors in the King's Chapel graveyard and referring to John Winslow not as governor of the Plymouth Colony but as an Herodian 'Indian Killer' in King Philip's War, sacrificing the Indian king as Herod did John the Baptist:

> Philip's head
> Grins on the platter, fouls in pantomime
> The fingers of kept time:
> 'Surely, this people is but grass,'
> He whispers.[8]

Flanked on the left by their Indian victims, the Winslows are flanked on the right by the Irish who have usurped their city. The dead Winslows cannot see the present 'Easter crowds/On Boston Common or the Beacon Hill/Where strangers hold the golden Statehouse dome/For good and always.'

This recipe for public lyric history – the disaffiliated son rebuking with grim triumph his rotting ancestors – is one repeated, with variations, throughout the lyrics of *Land of Unlikeness* (1944), and *Lord Weary's Castle* (1946); it governs the narrative of *The Mills of the Kavanaughs* (1951), in which the Kavanaugh line ends with the descent of its last male into homicidal madness and death. If Harry Kavanaugh is the allegorical figure for American ancestry, his wife Anne represents modernity; their marriage is damned because Red Kavanaugh, Harry's ancestor, 'burned and buried child / And squaw and elder in their river bed, / A pine-tree shilling a scalp.' Harry had hoped that his marriage to Anne would

> renew the cleft
> Forests and skulls of the Abnakis left
> Like Saurian footprints by the lumber lord,
> Who broke their virgin greenness cord by cord
> To build his clearing.[9]

Renewal of the genocidal past proves to be impossible, and Lowell's implacably vengeful writing of history pairs Harry's modern mental collapse with the historical massacre of the Abnakis, thereby proving Lowell himself, ideologically at least, a predestinarian Calvinist of the very stripe he condemns, and a believer in causally-structured narrative.

This politically correct version of American public history-by-hindsight could not long appeal to a mind of any intelligence. Even Lowell's own strategies in uttering it speak of his divided mind. 'At the Indian Killer's Grave,' though it is partly modelled on the Protestant *Lycidas*, ends (most peculiarly for a New England historical poem) with a Roman Catholic representation of Mary twining an Indian warlock with her flowers, her 'whole body an ecstatic womb, / As through the trellis peers the sudden Bridegroom.' *The Mills of the Kavanaughs*, on the other hand, keeps its historical material Protestant, and places it under the Augustan control of heroic couplets and heroic quatrains; its mythical allusions refer to Pluto and Persephone rather than to Christ and Mary. In the narrative itself, a cyclic determinism replaces the myth of corrective and redemptive history dominating 'At the Indian Killer's Grave.' But in the case of both poems, the present imposes its reality on that of the past, whether by the poet's surveillance of the past through a Roman Catholic lens or by the poet's unclassical momentum pulling Augustan couplets and quatrains into a hectic modern enjambment. As William Carlos Williams said in his review of *The Mills of the Kavanaughs*, noting this prosodic paradox, 'Mr. Lowell appears to be restrained by the lines; he appears to *want* to break them.'[10]

There is a distinct pause in Lowell's career between these early allusive public historical poems – where the reader is expected to know intimately the history of New England, and the 'facts' are extrinsic to the poetry – and the 1960 publication of *Life Studies*, which, in its sequence of that name, dwelt exclusively on family history. Lowell had written to Peter Taylor in 1952,

It's hell finding a new style or rather finding that your old style won't say any of the things that you want to, and that you can't write it if you try, and yet the petrified flotsam bits of it are always bobbling up where you don't want them.[11]

Though Lowell here puts the problem in linguistic terms – wanting a new style that would repudiate petrified phrases – this formulation is the outward sign of an inward imaginative upheaval. Lowell then moves out of strictly metered and rhymed verse, a move that reveals his inward revulsion against his own past practice. Lowell began to read Freud with mounting excitement, and wrote in 1953 to Elizabeth Hardwick, 'I am a slavish convert. . . . I am a walking goldmine.'[12] Though his mother's death, following closely on his father's, sent him into a prolonged manic-depressive episode treated with Thorazine and electroshock, he recovered to write the reminiscences of childhood that became 91 *Revere Street*. In the hospital, as he later recalled, 'My bluster and manic antics died away. Images of my spoiled childhood ached inside

[7]

me.'[13] And he told Peter Taylor that he was writing scenes from his childhood:

> I want to invent and forget a lot but at the same time have the historian's wonderful advantage – the reader must always be forced to say 'This is tops, but even if it weren't it's true.'[14]

Lowell compounded his internal return to childhood scenes by moving in 1955 into a house on Marlborough Street in Boston, 'a block away from the one [he] grew up in.'[15] He embarked on what he called, in a letter to his elder cousin Harriet Winslow, 'a little ancestor worshipping spree,' in which he read the works of relatively recent nineteenth- and twentieth-century Lowells – Robert Traill Spence Lowell (the Protestant minister to the Eskimos after whom he was named), James Russell Lowell, and Amy Lowell, all of them poets. In 1957, his daughter Harriet was born, an event which encouraged him toward a family history that would be contemporary as well as retrospective.

Originating from the prose of 91 *Revere Street*, the poems of the sequence 'Life Studies' (in the volume of that name) were written, Lowell said, 'in a style I thought I had discovered in Flaubert, one that used images and ironic or amusing particulars.'[16] He may also have been influenced by what he would call, late in life, Pound's 'enchanted discontinuity' in the *Cantos*.[17] To Randall Jarrell he wrote, 'I've been loosening up the meter, as you'll see and horsing out all the old theology and symbolism and *verbal* violence.'[18] So much of Lowell's old manner was missing that Allen Tate wrote in 1957 that the new poems were 'composed of unassimilated details, terribly intimate, and coldly noted.'[19] By 1958, when Lowell sent off the manuscript of *Life Studies* to his publisher, he could write to Peter Taylor that he was in 'the fine mood of an author with a new style and feel nothing else I've ever done counts.'[20]

Lowell's close friend, John Thompson, reviewing *Life Studies*, wrote that Lowell's 'new poems have abandoned the myths of eschatology and the masks of heroes,'[21] but, as we shall see, the abandon of public history was not permanent.

Although political history does occasionally appear in some of the poems of *Life Studies*, it is tucked into personal history, as though only there could it have continuing force. In the elegy 'Ford Madox Ford,' Lloyd George appears, but only as a golf partner to Ford; and World War I is mentioned only as the cause of Ford's novel *The Good Soldier*. In 'For George Santayana,' World War II is simply the source of 'bus-loads of souvenir-deranged G.I.'s' who come to visit Santayana. Stalin turns up in an incidental drunken quotation in 'To Delmore Schwartz.' World War I is dimly seen again, this time as the source of posters in a summer cabin in 'My Last Afternoon with Uncle Devereux Winslow.' Pre-Revolutionary American history and the Civil War are mentioned briefly and tangentially in 'Dunbarton'; Napoleon is glancingly invoked in 'Commander Lowell' and 'Sailing Home from Rapallo.' And in the moment that reveals the motive behind this sidelining of conventional 'history,' Lowell shows us himself spurning the 'Ancien Régime' of his grandfather's reign: at his grandfather's farm,

> I hold an *Illustrated London News* –;
> disloyal still,
> I doodle handlebar
> mustaches on the last Russian Czar.
>
> (75)

The graffito is a new way of being 'disloyal.' Instead of his earlier fashion of countering Calvinist history with a Catholic anti-myth equalling it in sublimity (and therefore of identical psychic import) Lowell now resorts to buffoonery, putting the old régime not under erasure but under satiric decoration. Lowell was unfailingly creative in life in inventing ways of being disloyal to family propriety – ways ranging from his juvenile misbehavior in the Boston Public Garden, through his three-year deviation into Roman Catholicism, to his association with 'unsuitable' girlfriends. He was equally inventive in being disloyal in art, as in his rude wrenchings of Augustan metrics. By the time of *Life Studies*, his reading of Freud, reinforced by psychotherapy, seems to have suggested to him that the only truly important history was family history, private history – the ultimate source, after all, of the driven and grand behavior of his historical heroes. The fascination of an intimate history overcame and seemed to replace Lowell's previous addiction to public history – and when reviewers reproached *Life Studies* for its 'anecdotal' quality and its 'trivial' concerns, their disappointment arose chiefly because they had expected, from Lowell, large issues and historical weight. After all, it was the powerful historical poems of *Lord Weary's Castle* that had won Lowell the Pulitzer Prize.

What was the substance of the imaginative upheaval that led, in the fifties, to Lowell's concentration on personal history? A disgust for one's former self and the creation of a new style are inextricably twinned phenomena, and they measure each other. We might begin to get at Lowell's state of mind by noticing that a poem in *Life Studies* is apt to begin with someone or something other than the authorial 'I':

They're altogether otherworldly now. . . . (74)

The night attendant, a B.U. sophomore. . . . (87)

Your nurse could only speak Italian. . . . (83)

Poor sheepish plaything, / . . . my Father's cottage. . . .(82)

At Beverly Farms, a portly, uncomfortable boulder / bulked in the garden's center. . . . (79)

Gone now the baby's nurse. . . . (89)

Nautilus Island's hermit / heiress still lives through winter in her
Spartan cottage. . . . (95)

Lowell's new history, we can see from these examples, begins
with the minor characters in the drama, just as *Hamlet* begins
with the two watchmen. In fact, what critics called the desulto-
riness of *Life Studies* arises from the impression made by these
off-center beginnings. History, according to conventional histo-
riographic expectations, should begin centrally, not at a slant.
Lowell's offense is compounded by the fact that the endings of
these private histories are, it would seem, as inconclusive as
the beginnings are oblique: a doodling of mustaches on a
photograph, the quoting of an inscription from the flyleaf of a
book, the misspelling of the family name on a coffin, a con-
sciousness drifting in the sheepish calm of lost connections,
the rooting of a skunk's snout in sour cream.

What notion of history is implied by such beginnings and
endings? It is, of course, the notion of history on which the
psychiatric session depends, where a detail leads by free associa-
tion to other details, and the structure of a 'true' underlying
history is revealed only by linkages among those apparently
arbitrary perceptions that we normally ascribe to the poetic or
imaginative side of the mind. Lowell's Hawthorne, in the poem
of that name in the volume *For the Union Dead*, articulates
Lowell's new conviction of the importance to authentic history
of the fragmentary and the 'insignificant':

> you'll see him with his head
> bent down, brooding, brooding,
> eyes fixed on some chip,
> some stone, some common plant,

the commonest thing,
as if it were the clue.
The disturbed eyes rise,
furtive, foiled, dissatisfied
from meditation on the true
and insignificant.

(119)

When Lowell, in his youth, wanted to write about the public Calvinist history of New England, he found a way to incorporate history into lyric by speaking as a Hopkinsian Roman Catholic sternly rebuking a finished past. Now that it is his ongoing personal history that concerns him in 'Life Studies,' he must find some vantage point from which to tell *it*, and he must discover, as well, a level of utterance suitable to his new persona, the analysand, rather than to the denunciatory prophet. One of his discoveries is a detached mildness of tone: this Flaubertian tone is desperately at variance with the scandalous truths that it chronicles – truths of the elder Lowells' unhappy marriage, of Charlotte Lowell's seductive co-opting of her son, of Robert Lowell Senior's business failures, of the poet's own madness. Lowell's second discovery in 'Life Studies' is the ironic terseness of understatement. Even the worst, most central, facts of the poems are comically or ironically phrased: 'Mother travelled first-class in the hold'; 'This is the house for the "mentally ill"'; 'You face ... the kingdom of the mad – its hackneyed speech, its homicidal eye.' We see, now, the 'recipe' for history as 'Life Studies' understands it: an off-center beginning, a dispassionate tone, a gaze wide enough to take in bystanders as well as the protagonist; at closure, a decrescendo in lieu of eschatological fire; throughout, a dryly comic sense of the disproportion between human aims and life's events. The assumed inconsequentiality of the lyric protagonist is central to all these strategies of private history.

[12]

In 'Life Studies,' Lowell replaced the Christian emphasis on the immortal consequence of choice for the destiny of the individual soul with the ironic and necessitarian investigative temper of Freud. The collection of random data – the chip, the stone, the plant – which may be made to yield symbolic significance now seems more fruitful than the master-narrative of salvific history into which one may fit one's own dramatic tale. Structurally speaking, the new poems show an initial wide scan of social data-gathering: in 'Skunk Hour' (95–96) for instance, the remarks on the hermit heiress, the summer millionaire, and the fairy decorator precede any remark about the self. Though the poem eventually focuses on the protagonist ('I myself am hell'), it then widens out again to the symbolic environment, as a mother skunk and her column of kittens take over the rule of Castine from its exhausted New England gentry and their summer hangers-on. The structure of poetic self-history thus mirrors the structure of the therapeutic hour: the random Castine snapshots of the opening are made to focus in on a revelatory personal scene, which is then interpreted symbolically and projected out on a grander social scale.

It was not to be expected, however, that public history, the obsession of his youth, should forever recede from Lowell's poetry. Asked to participate in the Boston Arts Festival in 1960, Lowell delivered 'For the Union Dead' (135–37), a poem about a Civil War hero, Robert Gould Shaw, whose sister Josephine had married one of Lowell's ancestors, Charles Russell Lowell (who, like Robert Gould Shaw, was killed in the war). The poem is thus, though undeclaredly, a family poem; and in it, Lowell quotes from a letter that Charles Russell Lowell wrote home to his wife, Josephine, about her brother's burial: 'I am thankful they buried him "with his niggers." They were brave men and they were his men.'[22] 'For the

[13]

Union Dead' honors not only the person of Robert Gould Shaw, but also the stern and beautiful memorial bronze bas-relief by Augustus Saint Gaudens which stands opposite the Boston State House. It represents Colonel Shaw on horseback among the men of the Massachusetts 54th Regiment, a regiment entirely composed of Negro soldiers. By his own earlier request, Shaw – who had the right, as an officer, to have his body brought home for burial – was buried with his men in a mass grave after the battle of Fort Wagner, in which he and they had fallen. Far from criticizing the Brahmin past from the vantage point of the Catholic present, as he had done in *Lord Weary's Castle*, Lowell now criticizes Boston's Irish-American present in comparison with the New England past. It is not he, any longer, who illuminates the past; the past, with its noble but fading light, now illuminates the debased present, of which he is a part.

But this thematic change with respect to history is of less consequence for Lowell's poetry than his structural changes. 'At the Indian Killer's Grave' had begun at its central site and with its central dead:

> Behind King's Chapel what the earth has kept
> Whole from the jerking noose of time extends
> Its dark enigma to Jehoshaphat.
>
> (24)

And the poem ended, as I have said, with the eschatological hope enclosed in Mary's 'ecstatic womb.' 'For the Union Dead,' by contrast, is organized according to what I have called the Freudian scheme of apparently irrelevant detail, free association, a dawning focus of significance, and a final symbolic environmental broadening. But this scheme is now applied to the matter of public history rather than of private therapy. The poem does not reach its real time of opening until its eleventh line: 'One morning last March,/I pressed against the new ... fence on the Boston Common,' watching 'yellow dinosaur steamshovels ... gouge their underworld garage.' Pressing his face against the fence, and imagining the sacrilegious machines as predatory amphibians, the poet is reminded, in Proustian fashion, of how he pressed his nose as a child to the glass of the South Boston Aquarium as he watched the fish behind the glass. He reflects that the Aquarium is closed now (as South Boston has become the Irish Catholic enclave of Boston, deserted by its former old Boston inhabitants), and he regrets the loss of a piece of his childhood. The actual chronological sequence of this autobiographical narrative – adult's face against fence, recollection of nose against glass, regret for lost Protestant Boston – is reversed in the poem as we have it, which begins with the apparently irrelevant remark, 'The old South Boston Aquarium stands/in a Sahara of snow now.' Gradually we creep from childhood toward the present: 'Once my nose crawled like a snail on the glass. ... / I often sigh still/for the ... kingdom/of the fish and reptile.' And then, finally, 'One morning last March,/I pressed against the ... fence on the Boston Common.' Only at this point does Lowell begin the indictment of those who have sanctioned the gouging out of the underground garage beneath the Boston Common; and only after that, at last, does he begin the description of the Saint Gaudens bas-relief, arriving finally at the historical hero of the poem, a present-tense, 'immortal,' Shaw:

> He has an angry wrenlike vigilance,
> a greyhound's gentle tautness;
> he seems to wince at pleasure,
> and suffocate for privacy.

Shaw's immortality is generalized and yet weakened, as it

[15]

spreads to the present-tense dozing posture of commemorative statues of other Union soldiers:

> wasp-waisted, they doze over muskets
> and muse through their sideburns. . . .

Lowell now conceives of the events of public history as existing solely in commemorative art, on the one hand, and metaphysical 'immortality,' like that of Shaw, on the other. Past deeds of war have vanished into these aesthetic and virtual forms, Whitmanian eidólons produced by past artists and possessed by their present audience. With the disappearance of history as firm past reality, the poem tails off into the abjectness of a Boston now ruled by the immigrant Irish, who, like the skunks of Castine, have taken over territory formerly belonging to the Lowells and their kind. The Irish have defaced the historical Common on which Emerson had his transcendental vision; they have undermined the State House and the Saint Gaudens relief in order to build a parking garage; they have abandoned civic responsibility in letting the Aquarium decline; everywhere, reduced to the synecdoche of their vulgar automobiles, their 'savage servility/slides by on grease.' Lowell's anti-Irish statement, though covert here (as it was not in 'At the Indian Killer's Grave') shows a new, commercialized history replacing an old ethical history. The bas-relief shakes, and the statues 'grow slimmer and younger each year' so that they will, if the process continues, eventually disappear altogether (a prophecy we see fulfilled in Lowell's last book, *Day by Day*). Christian language, the 'Rock of Ages,' is debased to gross advertisement, heartless in its appropriation of Hiroshima for commercial purposes. What saves the poem from Pharisaic superiority is the speaker's own confessed participation in the degradation he so scathingly observes: 'When I crouch' – he says as he offers the most startling image in the poem – 'When I crouch to my television set,/The drained faces of Negro school-children rise like balloons.'

Lowell has now realized that the inner life, even that of a prophet, cannot remain immune from the corruption it describes. The savage servility he observes, if it is that of the Irish politicians turning Boston into one long financial and ethical scandal, is also that of the poet, representing old Boston, servilely crouching to his television set as the savagery of long-standing segregation victimizes Negro children in the white Protestant South – as though Shaw and the men of the Massachusetts 54th had died for nothing. Lowell's self-incrimination is a sign of sanity; when he was ill, he was tyrannical and monomaniacal, considering America 'the Roman Empire,'[23] no doubt because he was nicknamed after Caligula the Emperor. Lowell is still using the lens of his own inner life through which to see Boston's history, but now he knows that he sees through a glass darkly. The prophet has vanished; it is a sinner that speaks.

By 1963, in a letter to Randall Jarrell resembling the 1952 letter to Peter Taylor, Lowell says irritably that 'each new poem confronts me with the old familiar legions of my old tricks and accents'; and a year later, in 1964, he told Jarrell that he sometimes found, in the style of the volume *For the Union Dead*, a 'mean tameness and sour montony [*sic*] which I detest.'[24] A few years later, in 1967, contemporary history began to press hard on Lowell with the commencement of the Vietnam War, which induced him to reconsider the public historical sublime. *Near the Ocean* (1967) and *Notebook 1967–68* (1969) show Lowell taking two different approaches to public history. In the Marvellian couplets of *Near the Ocean*, he writes mostly as a sardonic commentator on war, admiring modern improvements in military technology while conceding that nothing really changes: in the defeat of the Philistines, after all, the Israelites, savagely circumcising their enemies, piled up 'a million foreskins stacked like trash' (143). This phrase represents a perilous return to a tone of dismissive brutality that was one of Lowell's early staples for scenes of historical violence. Remembering his own repudiation of that youthful style as a crude resort useless to intelligence, the poet stands back from his vision of 'man thinning out his kind' to speak with more detachment as he utters a world-historical elegy which subsides into *abba* Tennysonian echo:

> Pity the planet, all joy gone
> from this sweet volcanic cone;
> peace to our children when they fall
> in small war on the heels of small
> war – until the end of time
> to police the earth, a ghost
> orbiting forever lost
> in our monotonous sublime.
>
> (144)

It is an astonishing moment, as we see the poet who in 'Life Studies' had wholly abjured the sublime, now admitting its claim while deploring its monotonous historical repetitiveness. It is the very air we breathe, our 'monotonous sublime,' in which the posthumous earth – in reality, the posthumous-feeling poet – must nonetheless continue to turn, repetitively, 'policed' by weary self-chronicling. For all its elegance of phrasing, Lowell's stance toward history here is adopted from a known quality in earlier lyric, one which owes something to Yeats's lofty spectatorial positions *vis-à-vis* history.

All this changed when lithium carbonate relieved Lowell from the burdens of exhausting mania and wearying depression. He re-engaged in political activism, even if in the sheepish way recorded in 'The March 1' (180–81). Lowell began to keep a journalistic account in blank-verse sonnets of the mo-

mentous year in which America went to war, an account that
he eventually called *Notebook 1967–68*. In the indecision and
chaos of the political scene, Lowell found so much to look at
that he grasped at a new opportunity of style, presenting
himself neither as prophet nor as sinner but as a journalist
engaged in slapdash coverage. In scanning America –
'America with a capital A' as he called it to V. S. Naipaul in
1969,[25] he once again came up against his old antagonist –
epic size – with which the lyric has always been manifestly
uneasy. 'It's beyond any country, it's an empire. I feel very
bitter about it, but pious, and baffled by it.'[26] The poems in
Notebook record that historical and political bitterness and
bafflement, but they put it (as had 'Life Studies' its personal
historical fragments) in the context of the poet's own day-to-
day inner life. 'What I wanted to get away from,' said Lowell
about *Notebook*, 'was the photograph of reality. It really doesn't
matter whether one style is better than the last. When it no
longer serves, you must adventure.'

The 'adventure' of *Notebook 1967–68* is forecast in its jour-
nalistic title and its calendrical scheme, tracing a year's his-
tory. The title suggests historical writing of a private, sketchy,
and adventitious sort, writing controlled by the turning of the
year as events unfold. A wistful look at a desired coherence
appears in the book's sub-sequences, appearing as groups of
poems with titles like 'Names' or 'Power.' These thematic
groups are outnumbered, however, by groups calendrically
entitled simply 'Long Summer' or 'Christmas and New Year'
or 'April.' 'My plot' (as Lowell says in the 'Afterthought' that
closes the book) 'rolls with the seasons. . . . Accident threw up
subjects, and the plot swallowed them – famished for human
chances.' Lowell has become the swallowing whale as well as
the swallowed Jonah. He adds, 'I fear I have failed to avoid the
themes and gigantism of the sonnet.'[28] The table of historical

dates appended to *Notebook* covers two wars (the Vietnam War and the Israeli Six Days' War); three murders (those of Che Guevara, Martin Luther King, and Robert Kennedy); several riots (Newark, Columbia, France, Chicago); and the Democratic and Republican campaigns of 1968. The book veers back and forth between two of its inner epigrams, the first less quoted than the second. When he writes the first, the poet has been contemplating suicide, saying, 'No, happier to live in a land without history;/where the bad-liver lives longer than the law' (*N*, 51). The outlaw cannot live life in a historical atmosphere, since history is, from one point of view, merely the progressive codification of social practice into law. Shortly after this repudiation of history, however the outlaw-Lowell concedes to history in a second epigram: 'I am learning to live in history./What is history? What you cannot touch' (*N*, 60).

Lowell, now fifty, has seen history continually slip through his fingers, as the raw events of the New England past have changed to an intangible mental reality symbolized by the Shaw represented on the Saint Gaudens relief. Now, in *Notebook*, historicity ceases to have necessary sequence, and becomes spatialized into a three-dimensional panorama of space-time. This causes the disorienting logorrhea of one-thing-after-another crossed with one-thing-superimposed-on-another which is the hallmark of *Notebook* as it is of Lowell's subsequent volume *History*. *History*, the Poundian offspring of *Notebook*, defeats its own attempts to categorize, order, or chronicle its raw material in any way that would satisfy a historian. Lowell's overriding aim in the historical sonnets, from *Notebook 1967–68* on, is to keep both ancient and contemporary history before him in one stereoptical view, characterizing both with the racy phrases of a modern journalist. Allen Tate has the 'cannonball head of a snowman,' William Carlos Williams is 'seedy with three autumn strokes,' a goiter expert 'smiles like a raccoon,' Napoleon's soldiers die with 'grand opera fixed like morphine in their veins.' It is a hit-and-run, slash-and-burn account of life piled on life, because its poet, having in the contemplation of death glimpsed his own 'futureless future' (227), no longer believes in sequence, can sing only 'the dawnless alba of the gerontoi' (N, 83). The absence of any personal future dooms this chronicling to its contemptuous indifference, its mortmain equalizing of any event to every other event, its third-person view of its Gerontion-self within the terrible collapsing perspective of juxtaposed death and birth: 'Now I am dead, and just now I was made' (N, 83). Against the savage sameness of everything, Lowell sketches the dizzying vortex of the confluence of everything where, in a single sonnet, several times and spaces can coexist – as Pascal, Mozart, Joan of Arc, Marian Anderson, and Ann Adden occupy a single locus ('1958,' N, 89) . In Lowell's sonnets, there is no Poundian phrasal pause between juxtapositions; Lowell's merciless syntactic log-jams allow no room to breathe. Time's 'festering fume of refuse' (N, 96) appears to litter the landscape with unhomogeneous piles worse than Yeats's old iron and old bottles: 'old tins, dead vermin, ashes, eggshells, youth' (N, 96). Lowell likes making this sort of 'category-mistake' (putting 'youth' next to 'eggshells') in order to destroy the very notion of categories, a notion which is, along with the preservation of sequence, the foundation of normal historiography.

The historical sonnets are repellent in their picture of a human chronicle all gristle and massacre and delirium, where sex and war are indistinguishable and the outlaw heart, after its few interludes of joy, becomes 'frozen meat,' its 'fast colors lost to lust and prosecution' (N, 101). Lowell's inflexible iambic Procrustean bed – five beats by fourteen unrhymed lines – to which the sonnets (with some exceptions) are confined, exemplifies the sullen law of lawlessness, the unwilling accretion and forced framing of calendrical accident, issuing from a poet convinced that 'home things can't stand up to the strain of the earth' (*N*, 141). A brief glimpse of the end of time – one that would have detained the young Lowell long – stops the poet only a moment before he descends 'back into contemptu mundi' (*N*,145). The sketch of the monotonous 'tideluck' (*N*, 148) of life ends nonetheless with a belief in 'the eternal return of earth's fairer children / the lily, the rose, the sun on dust and brick, / the loved, the lover, and their fear of life' (*N*, 156). And perhaps we can say of Lowell's interest in the choking superfluity of human event in history what Lowell himself said of Pound's ideological fixations:

All these various things were a tremendous gain to him; he'd be a very Parnassian poet without them. . . . They made him more human and more to do with life, more to do with the times. They served him. Taking what interested him in these things gave a kind of realism and life to his poetry that it wouldn't have had otherwise.[29]

As Lowell gradually reworked *Notebook 1967–68* into his 1970 expanded *Notebook* and thence into *History*, he redefined 'history' as public discourse, and deleted the *Notebook* poems concerning his wife and daughter from the volume he called *History*. But this reworking did not change the style which now for him embodied 'history' both public and private – the anachronistic style of categories melted into one spew – 'rivers, beer-cans, linguini, bloodstreams' (*N*, 151). Even the reordering of the events of one year into the Genesis-to-now chronicle of *History* does not change the style or the syntax of the individual pieces, which, however touching the occasional anecdote, exist as detached vignettes with nothing identifying them except the external fact of the year of their occurrence. The arrant and slangy modernity of style used by Lowell to relate events nobly told in Plutarch or Joinville declares that history is unrelatable in its own terms, and that the chronicler must rephrase it in the anachronistic and contemptuous tones of a modern commentator. At the same time, this commentator is not ethically supercilious or grandly prophetic, in the manner of the young Lowell. He has learned, especially from Freud, that Cleopatra and Charlotte Lowell may be more alike than different.

Only in *Day by Day* (1977) – another notebook, but with a dilating rather than a compressing name – does Lowell agree to chronicle the events of life *seriatim*, day by day, not agglutinatively through a space-time totalization. *Day by Day* offers the almost posthumously-viewed history of the decaying body, seen in the far-off perspective of someone looking through the wrong end of a telescope. Two poems (about himself and Peter Taylor) are actually called 'Our Afterlife.' The peculiar clairvoyance derived from taking a posthumous view of the history one has lived and is living – a view unavailable except in imagination – has not been adopted by any respectable historian, but it exists in life; we have seen it in the diaries of the conscious doomed, aware of their certain death. Lowell's own view is chiefly a view of misses and mistakes seen through the remote lens of obsolescence, without the energy of process and cruelty that rammed home the lines of *History*. The lines in *Day by Day* are phrasal, full of the cadence of contingency: 'We missed the declaration of war. . . . /In our unfinished revolutionary now,/everything seems to end and nothing to begin.'[30] The swindling British carriers of empire earned their money by using marked cards; now, as history proceeds to unravel the very life-texts it wove, they are 'caught by the marked cards that earned their keep' (*D*,41). 'We feel the machine slipping from our hands' (*D*, 31). The phrasal, languid lines would amount to elegiac history if the speaker would

[23]

obey the tonal conventions of mourning; but his regret has a parodic component: 'Did they think they still lived,/if their spirit carried on?' (D, 31). As Lowell 'cherishes [the] expiring chill' of his marriage-bed (D, 37), and finds his own autumn 'the autumn of the world' (D, 65), he sees the nation-state not as the locus of individual power or heroism, as he had in *History* in such sequences as 'Names,' but rather as a biologically-determined ant-state, 'a state/unchanging, limited, beyond our reach,/decadence, or denial' (D, 66). Political governance is beyond man; the ants 'are the lost case of the mind' (D, 67), a mind that had hoped for dignity and redemptive purposiveness, not only in private personal life but also in the life lived publicly and collectively. Though some of Lowell's attempts to find dignity in collective life, such as his act of conscientious objection in World War II, may have been 'manic statements' (the name he gave to that one), by the time of the March on Washington in *Notebook* his rueful and humorous account of political protest has nothing of mania in it. But *Day by Day* exhibits no hope at all for the collective public life. The formal result of Lowell's posthumous view of history is a structure of the collapse of the public into privacy, coupled with a comprehensive and intellectual grasp of life which is nonetheless, at night, menaced by surreal dreams from his protesting unconscious mind.

Though Lowell's long historical view in *Day by Day* goes as far back as the Battle of Hastings and reaches to the present as he sees the Shakespearean living garden of England 'parceled to irreversible wilderness' (D, 55), I will take as my example of Lowell's formal historical process here his three-part poem about Lincoln, 'Square of Black' (D, 32–33). In Part I, the square of black is a daguerreotype: Lincoln and his son Tad appear in a photograph taken in 1861, in which, as Lowell represents them, they stare into the 'blank ledger' of history, themselves 'its murders and failures.' Lowell retells, too, in the first section, Lincoln's prophetic dream of his own dead body. (For the moment, I pass over Part II.) The third part of the poem also contains a square of black: this time it is a 'little/ flapping square of pure black cloth' resembling a bat, appearing in Lowell's own surreal dream, and existing, like all life-constructions, 'only .../in my short dream's immeasurable leisure.' Lowell gives up on monitoring duration by his adjective 'immeasurable,' and yet he keeps fully in view the brevity which any objective regard must assign to human life.

In between the two squares of black – the first a daguerreotype solemn, historical, and significant, but stripped of heroism; the second a dream-image inconsequential, unreal, brief, the whimper succeeding the whimper-once-thought-a-bang of youth – comes Part II, in which the Freudian 'vogue' of dream-interpretation is dismissed, along with its companion-modernism, into the dustbin of literature:

> Dreams, they've had their vogue,
> so alike in their modernist invention,
> so dangerously distracted by commonplace,
> their literal insistence on the letter,
> trivia indistinguishable from tragedy.

This, the central passage of the poem, can be seen as Lowell's verdict not only on Freudian dream-symbolism and the 'commonplace' of 'Life Studies' but also on his monstrous effort to comprehend, in *History*, public trivia and tragedy inserted into one personal compressed melodrama. Like Lincoln, who was 'shot while sleeping through the final act,' Lowell will, he thinks, encounter death in the somnambulism of his last sketchbook. By dismissing the importance of dreams in Part II of his poem, Lowell removes closing symbolic portent from his Part III 'irrelevant' dream of the fluttering square of black. He has forsaken, in short, the 'Life Studies' trick of a conclusion widening into symbolic projection, itself a leftover of Christian eschatological significance radiantly bestowed on the quotidian. The structure of a poem such as 'Square of Black' – which anticipatorily, in Part II, subverts its own symbolic climax in Part III, and which tucks history away, in the person of the assassinated Lincoln and his incompetent son, in an image never returned to for symbolic weight – is typical of *Day by Day*. One of the book's tropes for this suicidal self-cancelling structure is the pleasure-house that, in a violation of natural order, predeceases its predecessor, the cathedral (*D*, 55). The 'collapsing/accordion' of the poet's 'receding houses' (*D*, 73) is another figure for the same organizing aesthetic structure. It is as though the ends of poems annihilate their beginnings rather than fulfill them. Each poem is less at the end than it was at the beginning, like a face 'aging/to less generosity than it had' (*D*, 43). In the most acute and destabilizing of these images, the poet himself is aborted at his death:

> My eyes flicker, the immortal
> is scraped unconsenting from the mortal.
>
> (*D*, 50)

At the end of life, one comes to a point 'when any illness is chronic,' and 'the wristwatch is taken from the wrist' (*D*, 73). The doubled appearance of the word 'wrist' here, in which the second occurrence of the word erases the first, makes life less than a zero-sum game. The despondent and helpless speaker of these abstract and brief chronicles asks, using the same subtractive figure of repetition, 'Why has my talkative/teasing tongue stopped talking?' (*D*, 111). Now that 'heaven and hell will be the same' he must 'wait . . . without the nourishment of drama' (*D*, 111). The relating of history has become a self-deluding act in which the narrator believes he is 'fearlessly holding back nothing from a friend,' while in actuality the reader/friend 'believes me for a moment/to keep up conversation' (D, 121). Lowell's nihilism with respect to the conventions of historiography makes narrative, as one word constantly cancels out another, neither accurate nor believable. However, Lowell's nihilism with respect to history does not extend to the different conventions of art.

What sort of history is possible in poetry once one has abandoned sequence, drama, climax, and a belief in the self-validating truth of autobiographical narrative? The deep formal and substantive skepticism of *Day by Day* is itself contradicted by the poem 'Epilogue' (D, 127), which reasserts the power of narration while identifying it with Dutch genre-painting, thereby removing it from the temporality of historiography. 'Epilogue' ends with a prayer for 'the grace of accuracy' that is sustained by a faith, based on knowledge of the art of the past, in the power of imagination to confer a 'living name' on human beings who would otherwise be 'poor passing facts.' With the grace of accuracy, the modern poet's snapshots – 'lurid, rapid, garish, grouped' – may be granted the nobler name of 'photograph' – 'writing with light' – and his figures may glow like those of Vermeer:

> Pray for the grace of accuracy
> Vermeer gave to the sun's illumination
> stealing like the tide across a map
> to his girl solid with yearning.
> We are poor passing facts,
> warned by that to give
> each figure in the photograph
> his living name.

However, the touching moment in which 'Epilogue' gets a second wind – when the poet defiantly says, defending his

own snapshots of history, 'Yet why not say what happened?'
– is followed, in *Day by Day*, by a coda-poem called 'George
III,' which is billed as a 'translation' from Sherwin's life of
Richard Brinsley Sheridan entitled *Uncorking Old Sherry*. The
last view of the mad George III in this poem shows him
'mercifully unable to hear/his drab tapes play back his own
voice to him/morning, noon, and night' (D, 435). Lowell,
however, could not escape the tapes in his head, playing back
to him, one after another, all his strategies for coping with
history, from *Land of Unlikeness* to *Day by Day* – all right, all
wrong.

II
JOHN BERRYMAN:
FREUDIAN CARTOONS

———

The most inclusive rubric, perhaps, that can be proposed for the lyric poetry written in America immediately after World War II is 'Freudian lyric.' Not everything falls easily under this label, of course; but many of the poets of postwar America found in the therapeutic hour (and its textual support in Freud's writings) not only themes for their poetry but also new formal procedures shaping it. Earlier, I mentioned this point tangentially with respect to the poetry, both private and public, of Robert Lowell. Now I want to argue it more centrally with respect to the *Dream Songs* of John Berryman – who also took up Freudian insights, but in a way conspicuously different from Lowell's.[1] (The same general point – that the experience of Freudian therapy generated new formal subgenres of lyric – applies also, in different ways, to the work of Sylvia Plath, Anne Sexton, Adrienne Rich, James Merrill, Frank Bidart, Louise Glück, and, somewhat less obviously, Elizabeth Bishop and John Ashbery.)

I have chosen Berryman because, like Lowell, he was notably original in his Freudian inventions, and because his *Dream Songs*, like Lowell's 'Life Studies,' is a sequence drawing, I think, on the successivity – one hour a week, every week – of therapeutic interviews, with their small anecdotal narratives. Berryman, like Lowell, had a good deal of experience with breakdowns and psychotherapeutic intervention; both poets were intellectuals who had read widely in Freud; both broke an earlier 'intellectual' verse style to invent a far more colloquial and quotidian sort of poetry (influenced, I believe, by the primal sort of conversation that takes place in therapy); both encountered a metaphysical void in leaving behind formal religion, and found the Freudian master-narrative, with its emphasis on the inner life, a congenial replacement; both saw, in the material of American daily life processed in the therapeutic hour, a subject matter relatively untouched by Anglophile literary conventions; and both followed the Muse of free association as a path to the Muse of lyric. However, while Lowell retained, for the most part, an adult and integrated self as the protagonist of the poem, Berryman made the great leap of using, as lyric protagonist, the shamefully-acting self of his mad or alcoholic moments.

'John, we used the language as if we made it,' said Lowell in a late sonnet to Berryman,[2] remarking on their mutual capacity to wrest language to their purposes, and on their unwillingness, after a time, to continue to write classical lyrics. The sonnet looks, with ironic nostalgia, back to the *otium* of pastoral:

> Ah privacy, as if you wished to mount
> some rock by a mossy stream, and count the sheep.

But the 'ebb tide' of life offers contemporary poets no groves, no sheep:

> The ebb tide flings up wonders: rivers, beer-cans,
> linguini, bloodstreams; how merrily they gallop
> to catch the ocean.

Both poets wanted to write the new poetry of the ebb tide of the unconscious, full of its unmentionable flotsam and jetsam.

Lowell was conscious of how much his life resembled Berryman's: in fact, in his elegy for Berryman in *Day by Day*,[3] Lowell imagined that he and Berryman had lived a common life, the generic one for intellectuals and artists of their generation. Yet one could never mistake a Berryman 'Dream Song' for a 'life study' by Lowell; though they both used 'Freudian' materials and even Freudian structures, Berryman found it necessary, as Lowell did not, to make a cleavage in the poetry between his adult conscience and his infantile and deranged, though chronologically adult, will; and he drew yet another line between these faculties and his integrated authorial self.

John Berryman was born in 1914 as John Smith. 'Berryman,' the name of his adoptive father, was assumed in 1926; Berryman's own depressed father had shot himself a few months before Berryman's mother remarried. Berryman himself was subject to manic-depressive illness, for which he was frequently hospitalized; and he was prey to an almost lifelong alcoholism so acute as to lead to seizures mistaken on one occasion for epilepsy. Though his illnesses perhaps kept Berryman from finishing long-range projects like his proposed edition of *King Lear*, they never got in the way of driven lyric production. The suicide of his father when he was eleven, his intense romance with his mother, and his repeated self-destructive thoughts, actions, and dreams were the recurrent topics for his various forms of psychoanalytic therapy; therapy contributed insight but could not induce abstinence. At fifty-seven, in January, 1972, after some weeks of painfully-won sobriety, Berryman killed himself in Minneapolis by jumping from a bridge over the Mississippi.

Though Berryman did not begin the *Dream Songs* until middle age, he, like many poets, was early attracted to the idea of an isometric sequence: his first poetic work was four

Petrarchan sonnets written at nineteen, in 1934, for his mother's birthday.[4] Then, in the late forties, Berryman wrote the Petrarchan *Sonnets to Chris*. When he published these as *Berryman's Sonnets* in 1967, he prefaced them with a poem written in the three-stanza form of a Dream Song: in it, we can see the cartoon-humor which distinguishes the sequence of the *Dream Songs* from Berryman's earlier, more earnestly Petrarchan conception of a poetic sequence:

> He made, a thousand years ago, a-many songs
> for an Excellent lady, wif whom he was in wuv.[5]

The impulse to cartoon psychic experience appears – in this example of Berryman's unmistakable late style – not only in the initial hyperbole for the length of time passed, but also in the childlike enumeration 'a-many,' in the honorific capitalization of 'Excellent,' and in the baby-talk through which Berryman satirizes his earlier infatuation. These tropes give the remark the detachment of cartoon; and it is cartoon, as a genre, which enables Berryman to produce his most lasting work, *The Dream Songs*. Though these were begun in the fifties, they originated in 'The Nervous Songs' which appeared in the 1948 collection *The Dispossessed*. Six of the nine 'Nervous Songs' are eighteen-line, three-stanza poems, prototypes – though they rhyme differently – of the eighteen-line, three-stanza *Dream Songs*; and the last 'Nervous Song' looks forward to *The Dream Songs* as it declares that 'The friends my innocence cherished, and you and I' are 'Analysands all, and the rest ought to be.'[6]

The Dream Songs, 385 of them in the 1969 volume by that name, and others subsequently published, gave American poetry one of those rare jolts onward that compel lasting attention. It is important to remember, as Berryman said, that the poem is essentially about an imaginary character (not the poet, not me) named Henry, a white American in early middle age sometimes in blackface, who has suffered an irreversible loss and talks about himself sometimes in the first person, sometimes in the third, sometimes even in the second; he has a friend, never named, who addresses him as Mr Bones and variants thereof.[7]

Though it is tempting to characterize the two protagonists of *The Dream Songs* – the 'imaginary character' Henry and his nameless 'friend' – by the words of faculty psychology – 'intellect' for the friend, and 'will' for the irrepressible Henry, a much better fit comes if we speak loosely of the two protagonists of *The Dream Songs* as Superego and Id. Yet, though the second of these two names fits the anarchic protagonist Henry reasonably well, the unnamed Friend, representing both common sense and conscience, does not exhibit the irrationality and sadism of the Freudian Superego, though he utters the reproaches proper to it. He could more properly, perhaps, be called Conscience, like something out of a medieval Christian allegory. In fact, it is the very crossing of the Christian model of the Friend with the Freudian model generating Henry that makes *The Dream Songs* an original book; two great schemes of Western thought, the religious and the psychoanalytic, contend for Berryman's soul in a hybrid psychomachia.

The fiction of the *Dream Songs* (first published as *77 Dream Songs* in 1964) is that its two protagonists are 'end men' in an American minstrel show. This common form of vaudeville (still seen in my childhood) presented, while the curtain was lowered between vaudeville acts, banter between two 'end men,' one standing at stage left, one at stage right, in front of the closed curtain. The end men were white actors in exaggerated blackface, who told jokes in exaggerated Negro dialect, one acting as the taciturn 'straight man' to the buffoonery of the other. They addressed each other by nicknames such as

[35]

'Tambo' or 'Mr Bones' (the latter a name referring to dice). The unnamed Friend in *The Dream Songs*, acting as straight man and speaking to Henry in Negro dialect, addresses Henry as 'Mr Bones' or variants thereof. Henry, the voluble, infantile, and plaintive chief speaker, is the lyric 'I' of the songs; he never addresses his 'straight man' by name. Henry's own colloquial idiolect (sometimes represented in third-person free indirect discourse or second-person self-reproach) is not exclusively framed in any one dialect, but rather exhibits many dialectical influences, from slang to archaism to baby-talk.

One can see that there is no integrated Ego in *The Dream Songs*: there is only Conscience at one end of the stage and the Id at the other, talking to each other across a void, never able to find common ground. In the early Dream Songs, the fastidious John Berryman writing the poem never enters the verse, and never interacts with either of his split under-selves. As he wrote about his Henry, 'Who Henry was, or is, has proved undiscoverable by the social scientists. It is . . . certain that he claimed to be a minstrel.'[8] Each Dream Song is (with very few exceptions) eighteen lines long, and is divided into three six-line irregularly rhyming stanzas – an isometric form one might associate, looking backward, with Berryman's debt to the meditative Petrarchan and Shakespearean sonnet sequences or, looking forward to the therapeutic fifty minutes, with the inflexible and anecdotal psychiatric hour. Theoretically, anything can be said within this arbitrary limit, but one has to stop when one's time (one's rhyme) is up. Henry, the Id, has a great deal to say: he is petulant, complaining, greedy, lustful, and polymorphously perverse; he is also capable of childlike joy and disintegrative rage. Henry's life has been blasted, as he tells us, by the suicide of his father when he was a boy; he is driven by a random avidity, often sexual, which he indulges shamelessly until the unnamed Conscience reproaches him.

[36]

Here is Dream Song #4, a farcical sketch of Henry in a restaurant lusting after someone else's young wife: this is Berryman's picture of the Id at work, checked in its lust by Conscience. It is a poem unthinkable in American poetry before the postwar Freudian era:

Filling her compact & delicious body
with chicken páprika, she glanced at me twice.
Fainting with interest, I hungered back
and only the fact of her husband & four other people
kept me from springing on her

or falling at her little feet and crying
'You are the hottest one for years of night
Henry's dazed eyes
have enjoyed, Brilliance.' I advanced upon
(despairing) my spumoni. – Sir Bones: is stuffed,
de world, wif feeding girls.

– Black hair, complexion Latin, jewelled eyes
downcast . . . The slob beside her feasts . . . What wonders is
she sitting on, over there?
The restaurant buzzes. She might as well be on Mars.
Where did it all go wrong? There ought to be a law against Henry.
– Mr. Bones: there is.
(DS, 6)

It is Berryman's gaiety of writing, his joyous blasphemy of traditional love-poetry, that wins us in this Song. The parodic aspects are several: the *planctus* takes place in a restaurant; the lady is reduced to her body engaged in the inglorious act of eating; she is guarded not only by her husband by by a comic superfluity of 'four other people'; the Petrarchan lover's cry of adoration is debased to 'You are the hottest one . . ./ Henry's dazed eyes/have enjoyed'; the lover continues to eat, and does not omit to notice that it is spumoni that he is, even

[37]

if despairingly, eating; the lover's jealousy makes him cartoon the husband as 'The slob beside her'; the lover's admiration of the lady's beauty suddenly descends to a crude interest in her buttocks ('What wonders is/she sitting on, over there?'); and the conventional *éloignement* of the lady takes on tones of science fiction: 'She might as well be on Mars.' The lover's comment is of the fist-to-brow soap-opera kind – 'Where did it all go wrong?'

The growling, resentful, truculent, unmanageable Henry is an enviable comic creation, and his repertoire of semiotic reference, old and new, is lovably various in both serious and parodic ways. We become marginally convinced, by such a poem, that the troubadours were Henrys too, and that Berryman is merely uncovering the unsalubrious, but oddly solacing, layer of psychic squalor beneath high artistic convention. And yet, at the same time, we see the negative of this truth: that even the lustful and coarse-minded Henry wants to call his 'feeding girl' by a name like 'Brilliance,' to see her eyes as 'jewelled' and her company as a 'feast.' These are all metaphors straight out of the love-tradition, and what is exhilarating in Berryman as a writer is the balance between the parodic and the ecstatic that he keeps alive, as he reveals both the body's abject yearning for idealization, and the mind's conspiratorial desire for buttocks.

But there is a third ingredient of desire in *The Dream Songs* besides those of body and mind, sexuality and idealization, and that is the desire of the conscience. The conscience clearly wants something better for Henry; but it appears in *The Dream Songs* as an alienated voice, speaking from the other end of the minstrel stage from Henry. The fundamental staging of *The Dream Songs* as a comic interlude in blackface with the rebellious Henry on the left and the taciturn and wise 'straight man' on the right has roots going back, of course, to the good and bad angels on the medieval stage competing for the soul of Everyman, parodically restaged by Shakespeare in Sonnet 144, 'Two loves I have,' of which Berryman tartly remarked, 'When Shakespeare wrote, "Two loves I have," reader, he was *not kidding.*'⁹ Nonetheless, for all its debt to medieval drama, Berryman's staging of *The Dream Songs* ultimately mirrors, it seems to me, the classic analytic encounter. Within the analyst's office, the client is free to recount his most shameful wishes or dreams, to become his own Id; and the therapist serves in part, as Henry's unnamed Friend does, as a blank wall on which to project behavior. And, like Berryman's nameless end man, the therapist is also a reminder of the reality principle. I will return to this suggestion, but for the moment I want to dwell on the two interventions of the end man in Dream Song #4. Both are in the service of the reality principle. The first intervention remarks on the delusion of mentally idealizing one particular love-object: '– Sir Bones: is stuffed, / de world, wif feeding girls.' This remark has absolutely no effect on Henry, who goes on ingesting, along with his spumoni, the sight of his unattainable inamorata. The second intervention checks Henry's melodramatic cry, 'Where did it all go wrong? There ought to be a law against Henry,' by the succinct echo '– Mr Bones: there is.' The 'straight man' duly has invoked the Mosaic law, specifically the commandment forbidding the coveting of another's wife. This remark silences Henry temporarily, because it has literally taken the words out of his mouth; this suggests that the other end man is an alter ego. (Berryman probably learned this technique from Herbert, in whose verse divine replies often echo or rephrase words of the lyric speaker.)

Successive sessions of psychiatric therapy may be seen as another form of the 'sessions of . . . silent thought' which generated Shakespeare's sonnets and other such sequences;

[39]

the identical length of each therapeutic session, over time, perhaps helped to generate the strict eighteen-line armature of *The Dream Songs*. Any change in the social order is capable of creating a new template for art, and 'the Freudian poem' was perhaps an inescapable evolutionary form once many American poets began, in analyst's offices, a sedulous examination of the inner life and the family romance. Henry seems to me the first full-length poetic portrait of the Freudian Id – regressive, petulant, hysterical, childish, cunning, hypersexual, boastful, frightened, shameless, and revengeful; but also grieving, imaginative, hilarious, mocking, and full of Joycean music: 'I have a sing to shay' (*DS*, 39). However, repentance and conversion – acts to which Berryman, raised a Roman Catholic, was always drawn in times of sobriety – required the sacrifice of Henry, to whom the poet Berryman was much attached. Henry was so much a part of Berryman that the poet could scarcely imagine himself as a personality without the responses Henry embodied. Yet the end-man Conscience – far away stage right – represented something equally genuine to Berryman the man, and to Berryman the watchful artist, as well. The unnamed Friend reminds Henry of what Henry – behind his coarse thoughts – already knows; and the Friend is unfailingly courteous and kind, even in his mockery. What is missing in the tableau, as I have said, is any Ego that could unite the two end men. None of Berryman's therapists or priests or wives ever succeeded in uncovering or creating, in any stable way, that mediating Ego. But then the Ego is fundamentally insusceptible to cartoon-treatment; and when something like the Ego begins to be the speaker in certain later Dream Songs, the zest goes out of them.

The most original poems among *The Dream Songs* invent, with enormous buoyancy, the Henry-dialect, of which more needs to be said. This is not therapy-language as such; rather, it is a cartoonish poetic equivalent of the aggression and regression permitted in the analyst's office. It includes baby-talk, childish spite-talk, black talk, Indian talk, Scottish talk, lower-class talk, drunk-talk, archaism and anachronism, mega-lomaniacal self-aggrandizing images, hysteria and hallucination, spell-casting, superstition, paranoid suspiciousness, slang, and primitive syntactic structures of all sorts – sentence-fragments, incorrect grammar, babble, and so on. Many of these are present in the famous Dream Song #5:

> Henry sats in de bar & was odd,
> off in the glass from the glass,
> at odds wif de world & its god,
> his wife is a complete nothing,
> St Stephen
> getting even.
>
> Henry sats in de plane & was gay.
> Careful Henry nothing said aloud
> but where a Virgin out of cloud
> to her Mountain dropt in light,
> his thought made pockets & the plane buckt.
> 'Parm me, lady.' 'Orright.'
>
> Henry lay in de netting, wild,
> while the brainfever bird did scales;
> Mr Heartbreak, the New Man,
> come to farm a crazy land;
> an image of the dead on the fingernail
> of a newborn child.
>
> (*DS*, 7)

Haffenden glosses the last image as deriving from Cervantes' 'Colloquy of the Dogs,' in which the witch Camacha of Montilla was able 'to cause the living or the dead to appear in a mirror or upon the fingernail of a newborn child.'[10] The image is made more plausible when we know that in an unpublished poem of the fifties, Berryman writes of himself as 'a sort of Don Quixote trickt out as Lucifer.'[11] Still, the rôle the unglossed fingernail-image plays in the poem is a surreal one, as though even the newborn John Smith proleptically bore on his own body the picture of his dead father, which as John Berryman (he punned on 'bury-man') he continued to exhibit.

The elegant three-part comic strip of Dream Song #5 – locating Henry first in the bar, then in the plane, and lastly in the hospital – gives the sort of emotional access to Berryman's extreme mood-swings that the gloomy psychiatric diagnoses quoted in Haffenden's biography cannot adequately convey: 'Cyclothymic personality ... Habitual excessive drinking'; 'After admission he became severely grossly tremulous, insomniac, experiencing some frightening dreams, and was obviously on the verge of delerium tremens.'[12] These late medical diagnoses merely record, in psychiatric terms, the disorienting experiences which formed the given of Berryman's adult life, and out of which he made, so vividly, the Dream Songs.

To emphasize the difference between the given of 'life' and the made of 'art,' I want to quote part of a statement that Berryman wrote down in 1970, as Step One of the Twelve Steps of the Alcoholics Anonymous recovery program, a statement virtually indistinguishable in substance from Dream Song #45, written years before. A comparison of the two will illuminate the language and cartoon-pictures demanded by the Dream Songs versus the language usual to ordinary expression. Here is part of Berryman's prose statement describing various past catastrophes and ending with hopes and resolutions:

Hallucinations one day walking home. Heard voices.... Walked up & down drunk on a foot-wide parapet 8 stories high. Passes at women drunk, often successful. Wife left me after 11 yrs of marriage bec[ause] of drinking. Despair, heavy drinking alone, jobless, penniless, in N.Y. Lost when blacked-out the most important professional letter I have ever received. Seduced students drunk. Made homosexual advances drunk, 4 or 5 times. . . . Gave a public lecture drunk. Drunk in Calcutta, wandered streets lost all night, unable to remember my address. . . . Wet bed drunk in London hotel, manager furious, had to pay for new mattress. . . . Defecated uncontrollably in a University corridor, got home unnoticed. . . .

Hopes for sobriety: a reformed marriage . . ., reliance on God: outpatient treatment, A A.[13]

No pious hopes or stern resolves appear in the comic – but ultimately tragic – Dream Song version of the same catastrophes. Dream Song #45 is a list-poem enumerating predicaments which at the time certainly *seemed* to be ruin (being discovered naked with one's girlfriend by her enraged father, for instance) but which proved, when *real* Ruin came, to be merely impostors. This Dream Song of Ruin preceded by its earlier impostors is verbally organized by two almost identical lines. In the first, we hear Henry's illiterate boozy remark about ruin, 'He thought they was old friends'; in the second, we perceive that Henry has been shocked into literacy by reality: 'But he noted now that: they were not old friends.' Between these two lines the cartoon-strip of successive pseudo-ruins unrolls, until it dissolves at the encounter with the real thing:

> He stared at ruin. Ruin stared straight back.
> He thought they was old friends. He felt on the stair
> where her papa found them bare
> they became familiar. When the papers were lost
> rich with pals' secrets, he thought he had the knack
> of ruin. Their paths crossed

and once they crossed in jail; they crossed in bed;
and over an unsigned letter their eyes met,
and in an Asian city
directionless & lurchy at two & three,
or trembling to a telephone's fresh threat,
and when some wired his head

to reach a wrong opinion, 'Epileptic'.
But he noted now that: they were not old friends.
He did not know this one.
This one was a stranger, come to make amends
for all the impostors, and to make it stick.
Henry nodded, un-.

(*DS*, 49)

The poem is a concise anticipatory version of the later confessional First-Step statement. But it differs from its prose equivalent not only in its shapeliness (produced by grammatical and syntactic parallelism) but also by its reductiveness: Henry and ruin, old pals, cross paths (as if in the successive frames of a cartoon strip) round the world; then ruin, old friend, mysteriously vanishes and a horrible allegorical stranger, saying in effect 'I RUIN AM,' fixes Henry with a toxic dissolution-beam, making Henry evanesce into nothingness before our very eyes.

Berryman said, in his National Book Award acceptance speech in 1969,

Both the writer and the reader of long poems need gall, the outrageous, the intolerable – and they need it again and again. . . . I set up *The Dream Songs* as hostile to every visible tendency in both American and English poetry. . . . The aim was . . . the reproduction or invention of the motions of a human personality, free and determined.[14]

Two main languages, as I have said, were then available to Berryman for the reproduction or invention of personality: the

[44]

Christianized Aristotelian one of faculty psychology, and the Freudian one of Ego, Superego, and Id. *The Dream Songs,* while availing themselves of both, cartoon both governing systems, as if it were only by distortion and deflection that some accuracy could be attained with respect to 'impenetrable Henry, goatish, reserved,/whose heart is broken.' (*DS,* 319)

The desperate uncertainties of tone in Berryman's earlier sequence, *Sonnets to Chris,* are a measure of what Berryman had to overcome, both psychologically and linguistically, to find the comic equilibrium of the *Songs.* In the *Sonnets to Chris,* he was willing to satirize his appetites, but since the satire came from within the same speaking voice, it lacked real comic distance and lapsed into mere incoherence of personal tone. Sonnet #17, for instance, includes the lines,

> Ever I passioned, ah
> Ten years, to go where by her golden bra
> Some sultry girl is caught, to dip my nose
> Or dance where jorums clash.[15]

And sonnet #73 is still more full of bathos:

> Demand me again what Kafka's riddles mean,
> For I am the penal colony's prime scribe. . . .
> I am the officer flat on my own machine . . .
> On whom the mort-prongs hover to inscribe
> 'I FELL IN LOVE'.[16]

These heroics and banalities of the inner life were perceived as such, later, by Berryman, when, in the Byronic move of the Dream Songs, he mocked not only his former passions but also his former poetic language. The Dream Songs, one must always recall, are written not by Henry, not by the courteous end-man Conscience, but by Berryman the writer – not the often sodden, cruel, incompetent historical John Berryman, but by the poet who never lost his respect for accuracy of language, and who eventually found a miraculous comic poise. And how clear-minded the poet is, savaging each of Henry's pretensions even as he watches Henry engage in them. Unlike the analyst-Conscience, Henry's nameless Friend, the writer of these poems is not courteous and kind: he is ruthlessly pictorial and relentlessly analytic, ever the fastidious and aloof artificer making something ludicrous and touching out of the dreadful given of life – his wretched illnesses and their humiliating manifestations in behavior.

Henry, as the perpetual rebel against the Law of the Father, is shown to be dogged by a perpetual and unidentifiable free-floating anxiety and sense of homicidal guilt (sometimes parricidal, sometimes sexually-focussed). Or, when the depressive side of bi-polar illness is ascendant in Berryman, Henry is represented as paralyzed by a pervasive apathy, an unwillingness to play even his own game. Here is the opening of Dream Song #14:

> Life, friends, is boring. We must not say so.
> After all, the sky flashes, the great sea yearns,
> we ourselves flash and yearn,
> and moreover my mother told me as a boy
> (repeatedly) 'Ever to confess you're bored
> means you have no
>
> Inner Resources.' I conclude now I have no
> inner resources, because I am heavy bored.
> Peoples bore me,
> literature bores me, especially great literature,
> Henry bores me, with his plights & gripes
> as bad as achilles.
>
> (DS, 16)

Berryman's debt to the lyric tradition appears in Henry's appeal to Romantic gestures – 'The sky flashes, the great sea yearns, /We ourselves flash and yearn.' On the other hand, in Henry's frame of mind the entire Western literary tradition, from Homer on, is of absolutely no use, and so itself becomes a lower-case cartoon in which Achilles' wrath is reduced to 'plights & gripes.' 'Literature bores me,' says Henry, seeing himself in his plights and gripes 'as bad as [a lower-case] achilles.' The Dream Songs visibly adopt certain features of the long autobiographical poem as we find it in *Don Juan*, which originated, in our literature, the spectacle of an impulsive and greedy protagonist commented upon by a worldly authorial voice.

Byron is at pains to leave almost nothing unmocked; but behind misbehaving Henry, behind even his unnamed ethical Conscience, there appears another layer of reference in the Dream Songs, a layer which is not Freudian, which escapes cartoon, and which puts the Freudian taxonomy of the self into question. This layer is mentioned in the unpublished blank-verse poem I quoted earlier, where, after likening himself to 'Don Quixote trickt out as Lucifer,' Berryman continues mysteriously,

> And then behind the Don there is someone else,
> Known I suppose to Sophocles and God.[17]

By the time of the Dream Songs, Berryman knows that this 'someone else' is himself the writer, silent behind his songs. Henry is invented so that the lyric protagonist can appear to be the deranged analysand rather than the cool analyst. The poet, inscrutable, writing the Songs, has now withdrawn to the invisible position of the Joycean author, and the stumbling protagonist, Henry, becomes the autobiographical vehicle. It is small wonder that Berryman was annoyed to find himself identified as Henry just because the external events of their lives matched exactly. Henry is a cartoon; and his author was

[47]

anything but. Where, then, is the author, the writer, in the *Dream Songs*?

The silent authorship behind the earlier Dream Songs manifests itself chiefly, I believe, in the occasional evoking of certain art-works, both Western and Eastern, which were prompted by a religious demand, and which combine spiritual depth with aesthetic refinement. The work evoked in Dream Song #73 is the stone garden of the Ryōan-ji temple in Kyoto:

> The fifteen changeless stones in their five worlds
> with a shelving of moving moss
> stand me the thought of the ancient maker priest.
> Elsewhere occurs – I remembers – loss.
> Through awes & weathers neither it increased
> nor did one blow of all his stone & sand thought die.
>
> (*DS*, 80)

The comparable Dream Song #29 turns to Western art, as Henry recalls a Duccio or Simone Martini profile of the Virgin Mary or a saint. Like the Japanese stone garden, this medieval profile – an art-object combining spiritual stillness with aesthetic mastery – reproaches in the way the socialized Superego or even the Conscience cannot. Its reproach is silent, not oral; aesthetic, not ethical; spiritual, not social or legal. Berryman sets his Sienese icon against Henry's obsessive anxiety and sexual guilt, and reproduces in #29 the anguished and irrational thought-processes caused by Henry's conflict of values. The poem begins with the stifling and perpetual weight that torments Henry's guilty conscience, and ends with a baffled sense of its erroneousness:

> There sat down, once, a thing on Henry's heart
> so heavy, if he had a hundred years
> & more, & weeping, sleepless, in all them time
> Henry could not make good.

Starts again always in Henry's ears
the little cough somewhere, an odour, a chime.

And there is another thing he has in mind
like a grave Sienese face a thousand years
would fail to blur the still profiled reproach of. Ghastly,
with open eyes, he attends, blind.
All the bells say: too late. This is not for tears;
thinking.

But never did Henry, as he thought he did,
end anyone and hacks her body up
and hide the pieces, where they may be found.
He knows: he went over everyone, & nobody's missing.
Often he reckons, in the dawn, them up.
Nobody is ever missing.
(*DS*, 33)

The cognitive dissonance between terrified conviction ('I have murdered a woman') and absurd enumerative ratiocination ('Nobody's missing') results in the obsessive and habitual 'often' of the insomniac reckoning. Henry would be relieved if someone *were* missing; it would make his conviction of guilt rational, and he could reconnect his split pieces. But this solace is denied him.

Behind a lyric such as this there lie the religious lyrics of grief and guilt written by Herbert and Hopkins. But although Freudian poetry is sometimes called 'confessional poetry,' one can see in the instance of Dream Song #29 that it is often precisely *not* 'confessional' poetry – there is, as the poem demonstrates, no sin to confess, and no way to make amends, no one by whom to be absolved. The therapeutic hour is concerned less with 'confession' than with an analysis – carried out by various means – of what is wrongly 'confessed.' Neither Lowell nor Berryman as modern analysands can ascribe to themselves 'sin.' 'My mind's not right' ('Skunk Hour') is not a confession of sin; and there is no corpse to confirm as criminal Henry's anguished guilt. What the Freudian poem does is to analyze states of mind, and without analysis there is no poem. Of course, the means of analysis available to lyric are not in all respects the same as those available to the analyst; but the aim of the Freudian lyric is primarily analytic, not confessional. In lyric, the analytic move is often, as it is here, a structural one. In Freudian terms, Henry's 'free-floating guilt' would be seen as the sign of something repressed, not consciously available. The structure of the poem, which locates the 'grave Sienese face' between the two stanzas of Henry's guilt, suggests that what he has repressed is behavior consonant with that austere profile, the sort of behavior he still believes in, if in an unconscious way. The repression of chastity, the repression of asceticism, the repression of spiritual gravity, are odd things to mention in a Freudian context. But for Berryman, the adult repression of his youthful religious Superego is as great a cause of guilt as would be, in classic Freudian terms, the repression of libido.

The Freudian poem supports the wounded soul, and does not accuse it; it lays bare the mechanism behind the guilt, and does not accept it as necessarily founded on fact. At most, it traces guilt or madness to its origin in family history, or to its origin in a pathological scrupulosity, or to a repression of one side of the self; it then finds aesthetic means to enact its analysis, and can go no further. It contemplates the unleashed primitive emotions and language of the Id without concealment, as we can see in Dream Song #384, Henry's fantasy of killing his already-dead father. (Berryman probably appropriated this idea from Yeats's play *Purgatory*, the exemplary modern text about ending a chain of familial consequences.) In this Dream Song, Henry goes to his banker-father's grave

in Florida, and lets his rage, hoarded from childhood, have its
lyric say:

> The marker slants, flowerless, day's almost done,
> I stand above my father's grave with rage,
> often, often before
> I've made this awful pilgrimage to one
> who cannot visit me, who tore his page
> out: I come back for more,
>
> I spit upon this dreadful banker's grave
> who shot his heart out in a Florida dawn
> O ho alas alas
> When will indifference come, I moan & rave
> I'd like to scrabble till I got right down
> away down under the grass
>
> and ax the casket open ha to see
> just how he's taking it, which he sought so hard
> we'll tear apart
> the mouldering grave clothes ha & then Henry
> will heft the ax once more, his final card,
> and fell it on the start.

(DS, 406)

The aesthetic problem Berryman sets himself when he de-
cides to write actions and discourse for his unmanageable Id
has been solved here, as elsewhere, by relying on broad
cartoon-like strokes. The Id is represented in several ways: by
incoherence of affect ('O ho alas alas/When will indifference
come'); by childish regression of action and words ('I'd like to
scrabble till I got right down/away down'); by interspersed
melodramatic nonsense-syllables of revenge ('open ha to see,'
'grave clothes ha & then'); and by a temporary abandon
(between the sixth and the seventeenth line) of end-punctua-
tion of any sort. The final tableau – as Henry in self-pluralizing
wish ('we') takes an ax to his father's casket, rips the decayed

wrappings off the corpse, and then drives the ax into his father's body – resembles in its components an episode out of Poe, but it forgoes Poe's ghastly ceremoniousness of action and diction: this is why the Dream Songs deserve the name of 'cartoon.' The reductiveness and garishness and violence we associate with cartoons – and do not normally associate with our 'sensitive' therapeutically-presented selves – are Berryman's startling comic means toward representation of his irrepressible Id. Cartoon-strokes enable him to render his life-*donnée* in literary terms, at the considerable cost of an occluded and alienated authorial self, concealed behind its puppets.

Berryman's early poems had been elegant and accomplished imitations of Auden, Yeats, and Hopkins, written by a literate and gifted man – one who had gone from Columbia University to Clare College on a Kellett Fellowship, who wrote fastidious criticism, and who was something of a dandy and a snob. It was not until Berryman acknowledged to himself what witnesses to his harrowing behavior in manic-depressive and alcoholic episodes had long known – that within his sophisticated exterior there lived an uncontrollable monster – that he made the great leap in which he invented a Henry-language and Henry-acts, putting Henry's Freudian dream-life into verse. The remnant of sanity by which Henry is contained is represented not only by the unnamed Friend but also by the elastic but generally inflexible eighteen-line container for Henry's labile self. And the dangerous identification between the existence of Henry and Berryman's ability as a poet is visible in the fact that Henry's sole means of utterance is song, as his sole medium of appearance is dream.

A trust in dreams as indices of reality, a trust in the primary and regressive nonsense-language of the Id, are new in lyric. Dreams had been trusted in the past as communications from God or from the dead, but Henry's dream life takes its authenticity, in the poetry, not from its message so much as from its nature as fantasy.[18] The poems are dream *songs*, and the principle of musicality has something to do, for Berryman, with access to the Id, insofar as it can be made aesthetically representable. The therapeutic hour gives at least as much weight to unreason and dream and childhood as to reason and conscience and adulthood, and *The Dream Songs* are massive testimony to that analytic emphasis on primitive, regressive, and polymorphous desires. Like psychiatry, however, the Dream Songs also recognize, through the person of Henry's unnamed companion, a reality principle, who often serves, musically speaking, as a counterpoint and closing cadence to Henry's outbursts. There is a law against Henry, and without its expression, the music of *The Dream Songs* would lack weight, variety, veracity, and what we might call a normative key to which their fractured atonality can return – or, in pictorial terms, a gravely stylized Sienese icon to reproach their cartoons. As I have said, there is another norm, beyond Conscience, governing the poems, and that is the norm of irreproachable art, whether Japanese or Sienese.

The Freudian belief in the importance of the trivial – from *lapsus linguae* to quotidian routine – allowed Berryman to make his poetry – in his youth remote, intellectual, and relatively inaccessible – interesting to others. His early, abstract Auden-cum-Yeats voice – ungendered, un-classed, unidentifiable as to age – spoke of unspecified subjects:

> You and I are not precisely there
> As [relatives] require: heretics, we converse
> Alert and alone, or over a lake of fire
>
> Two white birds following their profession
> Of flight, together fly, loom, fall and rise,
> Certain of the nature and station of their mission.[19]

At other times in the early poems, the talk is so vaguely allegorical that anyone could have uttered it:

The ship is locked with fog, no man aboard
Can make out what he's moving toward,
There's little food, few love, less sleep,
The sea is dark and we are told it's deep.[20]

In one of his essays on contemporary poetry, during a murderous assault on a now-forgotten poet named Howard Griffin, Berryman says that we can see that Griffin 'is not a poet at all, since he can't contrive to do the elementary thing required, which is to *sound as if he meant it.*'[21] In *The Dream Songs*, Berryman sounds as though he meant it.

It was not until Berryman composed *Homage to Mistress Bradstreet* that he began to find the idiolect, strongly influenced by colloquial American speech–rhythms, that he would eventually bring to lyric power in *The Dream Songs*. 'Poems should be read aloud until you get so that you can hear them with your eyes,' (*Poems*, xxxv) he said quoting Shakespeare in Sonnet 23: 'To hear with eyes belongs to love's fine wit'. It was when Berryman began to hear his own seductively sulky and comic inner voice, and to hear it in dialogue with – of all things – a black-dialect Conscience (Herbert's Jesus in comic blackface) that he could begin, with objectivity, to write the antiphonal music of the Dream Songs. Without the madness that sent him into therapy, he might not have found Henry; but without the analyses conducted in therapy, he might not have found the literary artifice with which to represent Henry. In a notebook dated 'Avila 18 Nov 57,' he wrote of 'my long literary & practical acquaintance with analysis,' adding that

in self-analysis one has to face alone what is difficult enough for the ordinary analysand who has[,] to support him in his agonies of self-discovery[,] the forbearance ('love') & experience & skill (timing) of his analyst; perhaps I should not have been able to do it if I had not had, rather earlier, the experience off & on for some years of what is called supportive therapy by a first-class analyst and then the furnace of some months of group analysis, fr. wh. I withdrew wild w. rage & writing better than I had ever done in my life before.[23]

Though I have, up to this point, emphasized the Freudian origins and cartoon quality of Berryman's representations of disgraceful and shaming behavior and inner suffering, I want to end not with his means of representing anguish, but with his theory of anguish, deriving I believe less from Freud than from Kierkegaard. 'The only true picture of the poet,' Berryman remarked in a notebook dated 2 Nov 59, 'is that given by Kierkegaard.'[24] Berryman's copy of *The Sickness unto Death*[25] reveals that Berryman marked the following passage about one form of despair:

This form of despair is: in despair at not willing to be oneself; or still lower, in despair at not willing to be a self; or lowest of all, in despair at willing to be another than himself.[26]

Berryman did not want to be the person he found himself to be, which fell far short of his perfectionist compulsions. His constant temptations to suicide, recorded in many notebooks long before the act, show him unwilling to be a self at all. Willing to be another than himself, John Berryman willed to ⇐ be Henry.

A little later in *The Sickness unto Death*, Kierkegaard continues:

Now when the self with a certain degree of self-reflection wills to accept itself, it stumbles perhaps upon one difficulty or another in the composition of the self. For as no human body is perfection, so neither is any self. This difficulty be what it may, frightens the man away shudderingly.[27]

For a long time in his youth, Berryman had been shudderingly frightened away from his chaotic and ungovernable inner self, writing the early icy poems of intellectual aloofness, with their inability to confide in the page. When Berryman, reading *The Sickness unto Death*, comes to the prophetic passage about how a poet might represent despair, he brackets it, and writes in the margin two sets of initials: 'S.K.' and his own, 'J.B.' Here is that passage, which begins with the dilemma of the poet who wants to represent despair, allegorized in the person of a despairing man who wants a confidant and yet is afraid to have one:

Poetically the catastrophe (assuming *poetice* that the protagonist was e.g. a king or emperor) might be fashioned in such a way that the hero had the confidant put to death. One could imagine such a demoniacal tyrant who felt the need of talking to a fellow-man about his torment, and in this way consumed successively a whole lot of men; for to be his confidant was certain death. – It would be the task for a poet to represent this agonizing self-contradiction in a demoniac man who is not able to get along without a confidant, and not able to have a confidant, and thus resolving it in such a way as this.[28]

Berryman invents Henry, the demoniac man, and gives him a confidant in his black-face 'straight man.' And even as Kierkegaard allows his intense analysis of despair to turn into the menacing little anecdote of the Emperor who kills his successive confidants, so Berryman makes over his biologically-given despairs into ever more ludic versions of themselves. The rapidity, color, distortion, comedy, exaggeration, and brazenness of the despairs of his divided self allow us, in the end, to see better, in high contrast, the sickness unto death beneath them.

In inventing for American poetry Henry's storms of colloquial rage, grief, and infantilism filtered through the lens of Freudian vaudeville, Berryman released the genie of American language from the bottle of his earlier Anglophilia. By giving his Conscience a black voice – even if it is a white face in blackvoice – he embodied, too, the sustained reproof that white America faces from its dialectic companion, blackness. His unruly poems of loss, guilt, and fear are thus, in the end, symbolic of a larger disorder than the personal. Finally, in their recourse to those exemplary works of Western and Eastern art which display the stillness of a sovereign and reconciled spirit, the Dream Songs remain their own severest critics, containing within themselves both the demons of the given and the seraphs of the made.

III
RITA DOVE:
IDENTITY MARKERS

———

If the primary *donnée* for the young Robert Lowell had to be history, given the aristocratic family names he inherited on both sides; if the primary *donnée* for the fastidious John Berryman· had to be the shameful actions of his Id, loosed by his chronic manic-depressive episodes complicated by chronic alcoholism; then the primary given for the black poet Rita Dove has to be – as for other black writers in America – the fact of her blackness. Any black writer in America must confront, as an adult, the enraging truth that the inescapable social accusation of blackness becomes, too early for the child to resist it, a strong element of inner self-definition. A black writer thus composes both with and against racial identity. The tradition of American black poetry (only partially recoverable) displays a powerful array of responses to blackness, from the heartfelt Christian promise of the spirituals to the dialect-recovery of Dunbar and his imitators; from the social worldliness and urban language of the blues to the steely anthropological elegance of the poetry of Jay Wright. The history of a poet like Langston Hughes, at last fully available in the biography by Arnold Rampersad, can be read as a lifelong search for stances to take toward, against, and within blackness – from early Whitmanian inclusiveness to African 'negritude'; from African negritude to idealistic Russian communism; from Russian communism (which turned out to be racist, too) to Harlem social commentary. Hughes's most candid social portraits of Harlem were, until recently, censored from mainstream anthologies, black and white alike, in favor of his more idealistic and mournful work; but, as we can now see more clearly, Hughes's social portraiture was almost entirely unrestricted, imaginatively speaking. However, this wonderfully inclusive inventory of Harlem life was restricted in another way: lexically and syntactically, it limited itself to language that the most uneducated person could hear and understand. For a man of Hughes's far-ranging mind and reading, that linguistic self-restriction was a sign of unquestioned moral commitment to the black reader; within it, moved by the syncopated rhythm of boogie-woogie and by the unembarrassed explicitness of the blues, Hughes recreated in the simplest possible words the blacks he saw around him – the faithless lovers, the pregnant adolescents, the yearning students, the practical cleaning-women, the weary mothers, the bewildered unemployed, the prostitutes, the snobbish middle-class churchgoers.

A young intellectual like Rita Dove, growing up with Hughes and Gwendolyn Brooks the most obvious literary rôle-models among older black poets, would have found her own inner life asking for more than their populist linguistic practice; yet she would have taken, I imagine, the stern commitment of Dunbar and Hughes and Brooks to a poetry understandable by all as a moral warning against a style cavalierly hermetic. I want to take up, as my next example of the difficulty of writing contemporary lyric in America, Dove's experiments in the representation of her inner life, insofar as that representation reflects on blackness. I will be neglecting, for the most part, the handsome poems Dove has written that do not take blackness as one of their themes – notably, her poems on travel, on motherhood, and on aesthetic experience.

Rita Dove, for 1993–95 the United States Poet Laureate (a two-year post that used to be called, more accurately, 'Consultant in Poetry to the Library of Congress') was born in Akron, Ohio, in 1952. Her father was a research chemist for the Goodyear Tire and Rubber Company, and she first began to learn German at school, in early adolescence, because she had been frustrated by the presence of her father's reference texts in German – the only books in the house she could not read. She was a National Merit Scholar at Miami University in Ohio, graduated *summa cum laude*, and went, on a Fulbright Fellowship, to the University of Tübingen; after that, she took an M.F.A. at the Iowa Writers' Workshop. She is now Professor of English at the University of Virginia, is married to a German novelist, and has a daughter. During the eighties, she published four books of poetry: in 1980, *The Yellow House on the Corner*; in 1983, *Museum*; in 1986, *Thomas and Beulah* (a sequence about her grandparents' lives, which was awarded the Pulitzer Prize); and in 1989, *Grace Notes*. The first three volumes are collected in Dove's *Selected Poems* (1990).

Ideally, I would turn immediately to Dove's notable successes; but because the problem of the representation of blackness in lyric is present from the beginning in her work, I must address her initial difficulties in travelling that path before I come to her poetically workable solutions. No black has blackness as sole identity; and in lyric poems, poems of self-definition, one risks serious self-curtailment by adopting only a single identity-marker. A young poet, not yet well-acquainted with the reaches of her own identity, is more likely than someone older to focus on a single aspect of self; and we can see Dove focusing in this way in her first book, where she attempts to school herself in black historical memory. She writes, for instance, a dramatic monologue for a female slave petitioning, in 1782, to be set free:

[63]

I am Belinda, an African,
since the age of twelve a Slave.
I will not take too much of your Time,
but to plead and place my pitiable Life
unto the Fathers of this Nation.[1]

(28)

Belinda has only two identity markers; she is female, and she is a slave. Nearby in Dove's first book there is another monologue spoken by a house slave, also probably female (29). In yet another of these slave monologues, Dove widens her canvas for the first time by speaking as a man; we follow the abduction back into slavery of 'Solomon Northrup/from Saratoga Springs, free papers in my pocket' (31). Dove (a cello and viola da gamba player herself) gives Solomon Northrup a violin under his arm to bring him closer to herself. She learns, through yet other poems, to find black personae who are close to her not only by their blackness but also by reason of their intellectuality, and it does not disturb her that they are men; such men are closer to her than a female surrogate like Belinda, who, though of Dove's gender, is not shown to possess those conceptualizing and linguistic drives that make a poet. Dove writes, for instance, about David Walker (1785–1830), a black Boston shop proprietor and pamphleteer against slavery, who slips his illegal pamphlets into his customers' pockets. His abolitionist customers sew them into their coat-linings, but when they are arrested, the pamphlets are discovered and subsequently read aloud in court. '*Men of colour, who are also of sense,*' one of the pamphlets begins:

Outrage. Incredulity. Uproar in state legislatures.

We are the most wretched, degraded and abject set
of beings that ever lived since the world began.
The jewelled canaries in the lecture halls tittered,

[64]

pressed his dark hand between their gloves.
Every half-step was no step at all.
(30)

Many of Walker's fellow-blacks in Boston can't see the point
of his protest; and finally, Walker's radicalism appalls even the
white abolitionist press. At forty-five, he is found dead in the
doorway of his shop.

These historical personae, taken one by one, female and
male, represent Dove's first steps, characteristically objective
ones, toward the representation of her own identity as a black.
She is not afraid to transgress (in choosing to use a male
surrogate) current feminist attitudes of political correctness.
She also transgresses the unspoken law by which a black
writer is dissuaded from calling attention to divisions within
the black community. A historical vignette from Dove's first
book, 'The Transport of Slaves from Maryland to Mississippi,'
recounts how, in 1839 (according to Dove's note) 'a wagon-
load of slaves broke their chains, killed two white men, and
would have escaped, had not a slave woman helped the Negro
driver [of the slavemaster's wagon] mount his horse and ride
for help.' 'I am no brute,' says the slave woman. 'I got feelings. /
He might have been a son of mine' (32). In an unbearable
conclusion, the slaves were recaptured because of the Negro
driver's loyalty to his white master, to whom he reported their
escape.

Dove is here willing to narrate, without prejudice, the Negro
driver's conflict between economic loyalty and race-loyalty,
and the Negro woman's conflict between group-loyalty to her
fellow escapees and race-loyalty to the dismounted driver. The
many faces of division within the black community are part of
Dove's subject, as they were part of Langston Hughes's subject
also. In her early years as a writer, Dove entered a literary

scene where both assimilation and separatism had powerful voices in their favor, and her first book shows, in the tragic anecdote of the transport of slaves, as well as in the account of the repudiation of David Walker by the Boston abolitionist press, her willingness to make her readers uneasy. Yet even the best of her historical narratives become somewhat stagy in their strained joining of the exigencies of plot to lyric implication. The lyric has not created the plot, as it should have done (and as it does in the best narrative lyrics); history has given a prefabricated plot, and the lyric has had to dance to its tune.

Even when freed of historical circumstance, Dove's 'slave poetry' exhibits a certain awkwardness in its wish to achieve historical linguistic probability. The poem ironically entitled 'The Slave's Critique of Practical Reason,' transcribes the slave's decision, as he picks cotton, not to attempt an escape; the slave speaks in a 'folksy' language that nonetheless unconvincingly drops into – or rises towards – complex vocabulary and metaphor:

> Ain't got a reason
> to run away –
> leastways, not one
> would save my life.
> So I scoop speculation
> into a hopsack.
> I scoop fluff till
> the ground rears white
> and I'm the only dark
> spot in the sky.
>
> (43)

Against these relatively unsuccessful historical excursions in a lyric time-machine, Dove's youthful first book sets sudden contemporary glimpses of blackness that are bravely achieved, like the 'odyssey' in 'Nigger Song' of six adolescents out on the town in a car:

> We six pile in, the engine churning ink:
> We ride into the night.
> Past factories, past graveyards
> And the broken eyes of windows, we ride
> Into the gray-green nigger night . . .
>
> In the nigger night, thick with the smell of cabbages,
> Nothing can catch us.
> Laughter spills like gin from glasses,
> And 'yeah' we whisper, 'yeah'
> We croon, 'yeah.'
>
> (14)

This may owe something to Gwendolyn Brooks's famous 'We Real Cool,' but it avoids the prudishness of Brooks's judgmental monologue, which, though it is ostensibly spoken by adolescents, barely conceals its adult reproach of their truant behavior.

Even as she was sketching historical personae and contemporary adolescents in her questing attempts to represent blackness, Dove was writing color-neutral poems. In fact, the best poem in *The Yellow House on the Corner* has not a word to say about the fraught subject of blackness. It is a poem of perfect wonder, showing Dove as a young girl in her parents' house doing her lessons, mastering geometry, seeing for the first time the coherence and beauty of the logical principles of spatial form. The poem 'Geometry' is really about what geometry and poetic form have in common; and its concluding adjectives, 'true' and 'unproven,' are crucial ones with respect to Dove's later poetry, which respects fact and objectivity in constructing a lyric self:

Geometry

I prove a theorem and the house expands:
the windows jerk free to hover near the ceiling,
the ceiling floats away with a sigh.

As the walls clear themselves of everything
but transparency, the scent of carnations
leaves with them. I am out in the open

and above the windows have hinged into butterflies,
sunlight glinting where they've intersected.
They are going to some point true and unproven.

(17)

As the windows jerk free and the ceiling floats away, sense-experience is suspended; during pure mentality, even the immaterial scent of carnations departs. The magical transformation of the windows into butterflies is perhaps brought about because the geometrical word 'intersection' – by way of the word 'insect' – suggests the wings of Psyche. The poem illustrates Dove's sure way with images, which are always, in her poems, surrogates for argument. She often avoids propositional proof in favor of the cunning arrangement of successive images, which themselves enact, by their succession, an implicit argument, true and unproven.

Here, for instance, from a poem called 'D.C.' (the 'District of Columbia' in which the city of Washington is located), is Dove's indictment of the city. She begins with its most visible synecdoche, the obelisk-shaped Washington Monument, a 'bloodless finger pointing to heaven,' its bloodlessness a figure for heartlessness. She ends with the Monument, as well, as its image lies reflected in the long pool at its base; this time, the obelisk is the cue stick of a billiard-game, 'outrageous' because of the gambles with lives taken in this increasingly black city. In between are other images – impartially threatening here, seductive there – of Washington:

[68]

A bloodless finger pointing to heaven, you say,
is surely no more impossible than this city:
A no man's land, a capital askew,
a postcard framed by imported blossoms –
and now this outrageous cue stick
lying, reflected, on a black table.

(22)

A passage like this helps to define Dove's imagination, which is rapid, extrapolative, montage-like, and relational.

The most interesting implicit commentary by Dove on her own imagination comes from a memory recalled in her fiction. The young woman protagonist of the story called *First Suite* has driven across the country to the school where she will be teaching, and arrives, exhausted, a day early. The school nurse tells her to rest on a cot in the school sickroom. As her eyes adjust to the darkened room, she takes in her surroundings, seeing first, on a nearby table, some cotton swabs, 'ranged in a misty circle around the barely visible rim of a jar.' Near the jar, she sees a digital clock. On that slender basis – a glass jar with swabs and glowing digital numbers – her imagination begins to work:

I could imagine the rest of the glass and the wooden sticks as they drew together in a perfect cone, then going on to form the mirror image of that cone, like a severe hourglass. The orange ciphers of a digital clock flared: 9:59, 10:00. I knew I would sleep fitfully until I had seen 11:11 – markings in the sand, reckonings. Four marks and a diagonal slashing the four – a numerical group. The Babylonian merchant drew his staff through the sand, eight bunches of firewood – see, I have forty bushels of fine Egyptian cotton to trade.[2]

The glass (because of the proximity of the clock) becomes an hourglass as its cone of swabs is geometrically projected into a mirror-cone, like a Yeatsian gyre; the hourglass suggests sand;

sand conjures up Egypt; the wooden sticks of the swabs create the eight bunches of firewood for sale by the Babylonian merchant, as the hospital gauze lying unremarked beside the swabs (but soon to be noticed) creates the bushels of Egyptian cotton. The speaker's observation of the digital clock-numbers leads to a counting obsession, which compels her to stay awake till the numbers will regulate themselves into perfect symmetry at eleven minutes after eleven – the four 'ones' becoming four marks in the sand, which are identified as marks made by the staff of the Babylonian merchant.

Some such idiosyncratic associative process lies behind most of Dove's poems. 'Association,' however, is perhaps too languid a word to use of this process, since it has strong elements (visible in the excerpt I have quoted) of obsessive behavior. Until something has been done to reality, some operation performed upon it, this poet is restless. Things seem radically incomplete when they present themselves to her, in life, for inspection. To make things 'perfect,' the mind must extrapolate the cone made by the wooden sticks of the cotton swabs until it makes the more easily 'integrable' image of an hourglass, itself dictated by the clock; the hourglass, then, must find its pictorial completion in sand; a use must be found for the image of sand, and Egypt is brought in; the clock must be watched until the numbers 'come right'; the gauze, in order to enter the Egyptian fantasy, has to be fitted into a non-medical use; the sticks of the swabs must undergo a change in scale and become firewood, and so on. The almost inhuman elation felt by the young girl at the end of the poem 'Geometry' can now be better understood: once the theorem is proved, an incessant anxiety is given momentary relief, and the soul is briefly untethered, relieved from the confining pressure of internal cognitive incoherence. All of the images presented to sight in the excerpt I have quoted from *First Suite* are in fact elements of such a 'theorem' and must be somehow put into a relational syntax by means of such processes as extrapolation, completion, adjustment, coupling, enlargement or diminution of scale, and so on. When they all achieve a mental 'fit,' the protagonist can go to sleep, even without waiting for the magical symmetry of 11:11; as she says, '11:11 clicked by unnoticed; I slept until the door opened.'³ It was enough, for the relief of her anxiety, to have conceived in her mind the point at which the clock numbers would be no longer asymmetrical, as they had been at 9:59 or 10:00.

Dove does not always achieve her 'fit.' Even in an ultimately successful poem she is sometimes misled en route, as she tells us in an interesting set of remarks on an extraordinary poem called 'Parsley.' In 'Parsley,' Dove attempts to investigate blackness by moving out of the the predicament of African-Americans, looking instead at an incident in the lives of migrant Haitian workers in the Dominican Republic, where, as the note (136) tells us, Rafael Trujillo in 1937 'ordered 20,000 blacks killed because they could not pronounce the letter "r" in *perejil*, the Spanish word for parsley.'⁴ The Haitians, speaking Creole French, could not roll their 'r's' in the Spanish fashion; and as each failed the test of saying *perejil* correctly, he or she was killed.

'Parsley' has two parts, the first a song sung by the Haitian cane-cutters, the second a depiction (in free indirect discourse) of the dictator's thoughts as he plans the execution order. Dove has spoken of her false starts in writing 'Parsley':

When I wrote the poem I tried it in many different ways. I tried a sestina, particularly in the second part, 'The Palace,' simply because the obsessiveness of the sestina, the repeated words, was something I wanted to get – that driven quality – in the poem. I gave up the sestina very early. It was too playful for the poem. A lot of the words stayed – the key words like *parrot* and *spring* and, of course,

[71]

parsley. The first part was a villanelle. I thought I was going to do the entire poem from the Haitians' point of view. And that wasn't enough. I had this villanelle, but it wasn't enough. And there was a lot more that hadn't I said, so I tried the sestina and gave that up.[5]

The 'lot more' that Dove had not said after she wrote her song for the cane-cutters turned out to be Part II, her eerily-imagined monologue for Trujillo:

It fascinated me that this man would think of such an imaginative way to kill someone, to kill lots of people; that, in fact, he must have gotten some kind of perverse joy out of finding a way to do it so that people would speak their own death sentences.[6]

In these remarks we can see Dove's attraction to obsessive forms like the sestina and the villanelle, but we can also see her principled refusal of that attraction when such 'playfulness' threatens to interfere with a more important part of the poem's 'fit,' its moral seriousness. We can also see Dove's inveterate wish to imagine and understand, if not to forgive, the mind of the victimizer. Poems of victimage, told from the point of view of the victim alone, are the stock-in-trade of mediocre protest writing, and they appear regularly in African-American literature. The position of victimage, and victimage alone, seems imaginatively insufficient to Dove, since it takes in only one half of the poem's world. That half has of course great pathos, and we hear that pathos in the song she writes for the Haitian cane-cutters. (Its initial reference to a parsley-green parrot in the dictator's palace remains obscure until the second part of the poem.) The cane-cutters sing:

> There is a parrot imitating spring
> in the palace, its feathers parsley green.
> Out of the swamp the cane appears

to haunt us, and we cut it down. El General
searches for a word; he is all the world
there is. Like a parrot imitating spring,

we lie down screaming as rain punches through
and we come up green. We cannot speak an R –
out of the swamp, the cane appears

and then the mountain we call in whispers *Katalina*.
The children gnaw their teeth to arrowheads.
There is a parrot imitating spring.

El General has found his word: *perejil.*
Who says it, lives. He laughs, teeth shining
out of the swamp. The cane appears

in our dreams, lashed by wind and streaming.
And we lie down. For every drop of blood
there is a parrot imitating spring.
Out of the swamp the cane appears.

(133)

As she does in this quasi-villanelle, Dove characteristically
opens a poem with an oblique and unexplained sentence. The
ineluctable reappearance of the fast-growing sugar-cane, no
matter how often it is cut down, is enacted, musically, in the
exhausting persistence of the phrase 'the cane appears'; but its
recurrent drone is sharply countered by the menacing appear-
ance of the 'General,' who, so to speak, will not permit the
natural (if enslaving) villanelle-song to continue.

The almost-sestina of the General has seven stanzas of seven
or eight lines each, and a single, detached, one-line conclusion.
It is too long to quote whole, but in summary it reveals that
the parrot had belonged to the General's dead mother, and
that in her village, when a woman bore a son, the men of the

town wore celebratory sprigs of parsley in their capes. The
General, deranged since his mother's death, and hearing the
parrot repeatedly call his name in her voice, feels that he, as
her son, is dishonored by the presence in his country of people
who cannot pronounce her language, cannot, with the word
'parsley' (correctly enunciated), celebrate his male existence.
The General, too, lives in the continual anxiety of the
obsessive-compulsive; his relief comes by killing. He haunts
his mother's room in the palace,

> the one without
> curtains, the one with a parrot
> in a brass ring. As he paces he wonders
> Who can I kill today. And for a moment
> the little knot of screams
> is still.
>
> (134)

He orders, for the parrot, his mother's favorite pastries, and as
they arrive, 'The knot in his throat starts to twitch.' He hears
the Haitians singing a Spanish song, 'Mi madre, mi amor en
muerte,' and is irritated by their inability to pronounce its
'r's':

> Even
> a parrot can roll an R! In the bare room
> the bright feathers arch in a parody
> of greenery, as the last pale crumbs
> disappear under the blackened tongue.   Someone
>
> calls out his name in a voice
> so like his mother's, a startled tear
> splashes the tip of his right boot.
> *My mother, my love in death.*
> The general remembers the tiny green sprigs

men of his village wore in their capes
to honor the birth of a son. He will
order many, this time, to be killed

for a single, beautiful word.

(135)

The General's sense of certain Spanish words has been perma-
nently eroticized by their association with his mother, and, as
obsessed with language as any poet, he kills to defend his
mother's honor. Rita Dove, in a feat of sympathetic imagina-
tion, enters the white dictator's mind, and conjectures a sinis-
terly plausible motive for the mass executions of blacks based
on a bizarre word-test. Dove's stanzaic imitation of Trujillo's
disintegrating yet fanatically circling monologue is a wonder-
ful piece of prosodic mortise-and-tenon work. The poem repre-
sents, in Dove's career, a dramatic advance, imaginatively
speaking, in the treatment of blackness. It also marks Dove's
continued watchful distance from pure lyric; she is nowhere
to be seen in her poem.

This absence is mitigated to some degree in the supremely
confident poem 'Agosta the Winged Man and Rasha the Black
Dove,' which appeared in Dove's next collection, *Museum*.
Though Rita Dove is, once again, nowhere to be seen in the
poem as a lyric 'I,' her surrogate is present as 'Rasha, the
Black Dove.' When Dove was a Fulbright student in Germany,
she came across a painting of two Berlin sideshow 'freaks' of
the twenties. The portrait, by the artist Christian Schad
(1894–1982) was painted in 1929; the title of the portrait is
'Agosta the Winged Man and Rasha the Black Dove.' Repro-
duced on the original cover of Dove's *Museum*, it shows Agosta
– his naked torso deformed by a bone disease that causes his
ribs and scapulas to point out through his skin like wings –
and, seated below him, his fellow circus-freak, a perfectly

[75]

normal and handsome woman whose only freakishness (in the Berlin of 1929) was that she was black. Rita Dove, herself black, found herself confronting Rasha the Black Dove of Schad; it is no wonder the portrait generated one of Dove's most gripping poems.

The poem is voiced indirectly through Christian Schad the (white) painter. At first Schad thinks that his own scrupulous and dispassionate eye is 'merciless,' as it sees and reproduces, in unadorned and unconcealed directness, the two figures – one medically marginal, the other socially so – set aside as freaks by his society. But then he repents, and thinks, 'The canvas,/not his eye, was merciless.' It is the exaction of his medium, the stylized accuracy demanded by the portrait-genre, that guarantees the mercilessness of his work. But at the close, as Schad comes to a final decision about the composition of the two figures, he changes his mind yet again:

> Agosta in
> classical drapery, then,
> and Rasha at his feet.
> Without passion. Not
> the canvas
> > but their gaze,
> > so calm,
> was merciless.
>
> (100)

It is the stigmatized figures, heroically and classically posed, gazing out forever at those who gaze at them, who are 'merciless.' True, the artist's eye, with its absence of distorting revulsive 'passion' before these 'freaks,' plays a role; true, the canvas which confers, in its recollection of the history of portraiture, classical drapery on the 'ignoble' Agosta also plays a part; but it is *what* is rendered through eye and generic convention – the socially-marked persons of Agosta and Rasha in 1929

Berlin – that mercilessly indicts German culture. As the young Rita Dove saw her counterpart – a Madagascan woman who could find work only by agreeing to dance entwined with a boa constrictor, and who was given the circus sobriquet of 'The Black Dove' in order to recall the old emblem of serpent-and-dove – she knew *something* had to be merciless. In deciding for subject matter as the basic locus for aesthetic mercilessness, Dove does not discount either the dispassionate painter's eye or the contribution of genre-convention to the movement of the brush on canvas, but she asserts that eye and hand have to bend their attention on deep and consequential things, and that those things must 'gaze' out at the beholder so as to compel a returning gaze coupled with self-examination.

It is evident from such a poem, and from its attention to a painting by a white artist of a stigmatized black woman, that Dove has thought hard about medium, message, artist, and beholder as they cooperate to make art. No black artist can avoid, as subject matter, the question of skin color, and what it entails; and probably the same is still true, if to a lesser extent, of the woman artist and the subject matter of gender. Yet if these important subject matters are not presented by a dispassionate eye and a trained hand, the result will not be art, and will not exert a gaze prompting the beholder to examine his own conscience.

It was Dove's next book, *Thomas and Beulah*, that won the Pulitzer Prize in 1986. The book springs from the history of Dove's maternal grandparents, who migrated North (each from a different Southern state) and married in Ohio. The life they made in Akron between marriage and death is the subject matter of the poems, written as two sequences, the first for Thomas, the second for Beulah. Dove solves the 'color question' here by having everyone in the central story be black; daily life, then, is just daily life, even though it is in part controlled by a white context appearing occasionally at the edges of the story. The question of gender is treated in the poem even-handedly, as Dove, who never appears in person in the book, writes in sympathy with both Thomas and Beulah, often reproducing their own sense of themselves in free indirect discourse. Dove no longer looks to the 'picturesque' antebellum slave record, nor to an exotic collective massacre in the Dominic Republic, nor to interwar Berlin, to revive history; she records instead the history, living vividly in contemporary memory, of the industrial and domestic servitude of two ordinary American people in the earlier twentieth century. Dove integrates here two areas she had earlier tended to keep separate – 'low' art as in 'Nigger Song' and 'high' art as in 'Agosta.' In *Thomas and Beulah*, she keeps the individual sequences as elegant in structural form as a *lieder* cycle, while letting colloquial black talk run freely through them.

The story of Thomas and Beulah unrolls through brief snapshots: the history of their children, for instance, appears in Thomas's four disappointed words – 'Girl girl/girl girl' (158). It is a common story: both parents work in marginal jobs for low pay, Thomas in the Zeppelin factory, Beulah as a domestic and a milliner; Thomas is eventually laid off in the Depression; Beulah is disappointed in marriage and exhausted by maternity; and finally they grow ill and die, still in poverty. But the male and female sequences are punctuated by the ordinary satisfactions, too: making hair pomade, attending a daughter's wedding, buying – at a church rummage sale – an encyclopedia with 'One Volume Missing,' *V* through Z – 'for five bucks/ no zebras, no Virginia,/no wars' (163).

From this rich double-sequence of forty-four poems (twenty-three for Thomas, twenty-one for Beulah) I want to take as my example one of the poems that omits the context of whiteness, a poem treating the life of a black person as simply one life among others. The poem 'Aircraft' depicts Thomas working as a riveter in an airplane factory, in what should have been the heady days of a steady paycheck. But Thomas is not happy, as he faces yet another morning of his work:

Too frail for combat, he stands
before an interrupted wing,
playing with an idea, nothing serious.
Afternoons, the hall gaped with aluminum
glaring, flying toward the sun; now
though, first thing in the morning, there is only
gray sheen and chatter
from the robust women around him
and the bolt waiting for his riveter's
five second blast.

The night before in the dark
of the peanut gallery, he listened to blouses shifting
and sniffed magnolias, white
tongues of remorse
sinking into the earth. Then
the newsreel leapt forward
into war.

Why *frail*? Why not simply
family man? Why wings, when
women with fingers no smaller than his
dabble in the gnarled intelligence of an engine?

And if he gave just a four second blast,
or three? Reflection is such

a bloodless light.
After lunch, they would bathe in fire.

(160)

The things that make Thomas unhappy here are not his blackness and his oppression by whites – not at all. He is unhappy because he has been refused induction into the army as 'too frail for combat'; and he is unhappy because women outclass him at work – they get the interesting work of assembling 'the gnarled intelligence of an engine' while he is nothing but a riveter of airplane wings. The only form of vengeance for these insults that Thomas can conceive as within his power would be to disobey his working orders, and to give to his rivets, instead of the prescribed five-second tightening-time, 'just a four second blast,/or three.' He merely plays with this dangerous idea, but even his telling himself that it is 'nothing serious' means that he has thought of it enough to repudiate it.

Why does it seem so extraordinary in American lyric to have a black man treated as an ordinary person, with ordinary physical and social resentments? Somewhere in the background, of course, Thomas's blackness tacitly figures, if only in his poverty – he has to sit in 'the peanut gallery' of the moviehouse. But Dove's picture of a mind that is occupied with induction-disappointment and gender-jealousy is both particular enough not to attempt a false 'universality' and humdrum enough to make Thomas like many other men, white as well as black. With her usual cunning, Dove presents Thomas's interior monologue in interlocking thematic snippets, concerning A) War, B) Disobedience, C) Masculine Fire, and D) Women. The sequence of these elements, abstractly rendered, would look like this:

A: Draft-board insult – induction denied
B: Thought [of possible work-disobedience] – dismissed
C: Afternoon brilliance of light, enlivening factory environment
D: Chatter of women, linked to grayness of morning
B: Prescribed order of riveting

D: Flashback to women in moviehouse, with Thomas longing

(remorsefully) for extramarital sex
A: Newsreel of war

A: Induction insult remembered
D: Defense against infidelity; assertion of marital bond
A/D: Insult repeated – women have better jobs in war-work

B: Thought of vengeance (in reprisal for insults) once again enter-
      tained – this time clearly defined as subversion of orders –
      but reflection is dismissed as

D: A bloodless light like the gray light of morning, time of the
      chatter of women
C: Longing for fiery brilliance of afternoon.

If we turn this scheme into a string of code for each of the five
stanzas, its DNA reads:

$$
\begin{array}{lll}
\text{1) ABCDB:} & & \text{10 lines} \\
\text{2) DA} & : & \text{7 lines} \\
\text{3) ADA/D:} & & \text{4 lines} \\
\text{4) B} & : & \text{2 lines} \\
\text{5) DC} & : & \text{2 lines}
\end{array}
$$

As the duration of each successive stanza becomes more con-
stricted, the tension between vengeance and insult – between
a longed-for masculine fiery glare and the actual gray female
superiority – grows. Dove fleshes out each of her elements –
ABCD – by tiny vignettes, so that each takes on characteristic
sensuous force; and she links the elements of the vignettes by
an immediate musicality of alliteration and assonance. The
early separate w's and wh's of *wing*, *with*, *women*, and *white*,
for instance, suddenly flare, in the third stanza, into a flurry of
repeated w's: *war*, *why*, *why*, *why*, *wings*, *when*, *women*, *with* –
eight words beginning with *w* out of thirteen successive
words:

. . . war.

Why *frail?* Why not simply
family man? Why wings, when
women with . . .

One can almost hear Thomas's frustrated stutter accompany-
ing his three successive indignant questions. It is not coward-
ice that makes Thomas draw back from vengeance, nor patriot-
ism that prevents his impulse to sabotage the firmness of his
rivets. It is rather the fact that abstract and 'bloodless' reflec-
tion is not natural to him; he lives in a world of work, visuality,
and sexual desire, not a second-order world of thought. To
comfort himself, he turns his mind to the satisfying masculine
exaltation of aluminum glare in the afternoon sun, as the
word *fire,* with which the poem ends, satisfyingly combats and
'replaces' the insult *frail,* with which the poem had begun. Of
course, if the two words did not share the three essential
letters *f i r,* the replacement would not seem so poetically
satisfying.

Thomas and Beulah represents Dove's rethinking of the lyric
poet's relation to the history of blackness. No longer bound to
a single lyric moment, she lets the successive raw data of life
(perceived over time by a man and by his wife at the same
epoch and in the same circumstances) become pieces for a
reader to assemble. The sure hand of structural form supports
each life-glimpse: cunningly counter-balancing each other into
stability, the tart and touching individual poems add up to a
sturdy two-part invention which symbolizes that mysterious
third thing, a lifelong marriage – lived, it is true, in blackness
but not determined by blackness alone.

This important discovery – that blackness need not be one's
central subject, but equally need not be omitted – has governed
Dove's work since *Thomas and Beulah.* Various poems and

[82]

sequences in *Grace Notes* (1989) have adopted this attitude, neither focusing exclusively on race nor excluding it from presence when it comes up. The aesthetic level from which this balancing of subject matter arises has nothing much to do, I think, with blackness. It comes from Dove's discovery (as she puts it in a poem called 'Particulars') that life exhibits a 'lack of conclusion,' and presents an 'eternal *dénouement*.'[7] For a poet obsessively concerned with 'fit,' with what 'Particulars' dryly calls 'agenda' – having one's 'second coffee at nine . . . / crying every morning, ten sharp,' – the recognition of the repetitiveness of that life-pattern makes the notion of 'particular sorrow' moot. The newly-learned 'secret' of life – that it lacks conclusion, is always unknotting what it has knotted – is the most devastating secret a poet like Dove, drawn to conclusiveness, could learn. 'Each knot of grief,/each snagged insistence' (*GN*,43) is now subject to being unwound; and somehow the poems will have to insist on the temporariness of their psychic states rather than on conclusiveness and 'fit' alone.

This means the abandon of the 'dovetailing' – and the pun is justified – which was, aesthetically, so enormously reassuring in a poem like 'Aircraft.' I think Dove is not yet sure what can replace dovetailing in terms of formal construction. But she knows, thematically, that exploration of un-dovetailed conditions and blurred places is what lies in store for her. I will take up (from *Grace Notes*) two examples of Dove's new style, both of which deal in some way with blackness.

Blackness begins, but does not end, a poem called 'Stitches'; the poet slips and falls, breaking open an old scar so that she has to be taken to the hospital Emergency Room to have the wound stitched. During the poem, she carries on a sardonic dialogue (in italics) with herself, first in self-reproach for carelessness, then in self-reproach for her instant intellectual meta-

phorizing of the doctor's stitching of her wound. In the begin-
ning of the poem, the tear in the flesh is immediately inter-
preted by the first, involuntary reference point for any black
person, the fact of blackness – which always threatens to be
the only referent for the self, closing down other facets of
identity:

> When skin opens
> where a scar
> should be, I think nothing but
> 'So I *am* white underneath!'
> Blood swells then
> dribbles into the elbow.

At the end of the poem, we meet first a witty set of metaphors
about the doctor stitching the wound (including a last mention
of blackness, black skin being seen as 'topsoil'), and then we
meet the poet's self-reproach for her automatic wish to trope
(and distance) everything, no matter what the occasion. Black-
ness is forgotten in favor of critical self-interrogation:

> The doctor's teeth are beavery, yellow:
> he whistles as he works, as topsoil
> puckers over its wound. Amazing
> there's no pain – just pressure
> as the skin's tugged up by his thread
>
> like a trout, a black line straight
> from a seamstress' nightmare: foot-tread
> pedalling the needle right through.
>
> *You just can't stop being witty, can you?*
>
> Oh, but I can. I always could.
> (GN, 51)

The self that hates wit, and utters the sardonic baiting line, is the same self that makes wit. The more interesting alternative self, emerging only in the rebuttal closing the poem, is a non-ironic one, always present but sometimes choosing, by allowing wit its play, to refrain from 'earnestness.'

That 'earnest' self is the self of most first-generation black American poets. It was first countered in a sustained way by Langston Hughes, who took on the wit and gallantry of the blues as an antidote to plangency or indignation. The 'earnest' writer-self behind 'Stitches' cannot any longer employ the sophisticated and oblique arrangements of the earlier artificer-self; and so 'Stitches' is told chronologically, in the order of its happening, rather than by the ingenious process of reflective faceting which organized a poem like 'Aircraft.' 'Stitches,' as it progresses, literally shows blackness being forgotten in favor of the more urgent inner aesthetic conflict between earnestness and wit. And yet by admitting that her first, instinctive response to a wound was her assertion of inner whiteness, Dove shows blackness as an ever-present, unsheddable first skin of consciousness, a constant spur to 'earnestness' against the aesthetic playfulness of poetic wit.

The last poem I will mention is one I perhaps do not entirely understand. It is called 'Medusa,' (GN, 55) and plays (I think) with the idea of blackness as conferring gorgon-status on a black woman. Sexual feeling is identified with an underground cave-like liquid darkness which the eye, another 'hairy star,' cannot reach, and is in danger of forgetting:

> I've got to go
> down where my eye
> can't reach
> hairy star
> who forgets to shiver
> forgets the cool suck
> inside

In a famous poem, 'I, Too,' published in 1932, Langston Hughes prophesied eventual justice for the American black – that he would be invited to leave his ignominious place in the kitchen and allowed to join in the general feast at the table. And yet, for Hughes, justice alone does not suffice. Hughes ends his poem with a vision that was astonishing at its moment in the thirties – that the aesthetic of America will change, and that the black body, which seemed a thing of revulsion, will be seen, amazingly, as *beautiful*:

> Tomorrow,
> I'll be at the table
> When company comes.
> Nobody'll dare
> Say to me,
> 'Eat in the kitchen,'
> Then.
>
> Besides,
> They'll see how beautiful I am
> And be ashamed –
>
> I, too, am America.[8]

Dove's 'Medusa' is a descendant of 'I, Too,' and embodies a comparable prophecy: that the despised Medusa, once she is seen and loved, will become a star (even a constellation) in that process that 'stellified' Berenice's and Belinda's hair:

> Someday long
> off someone will
> see me
> fling me up
> until I hook
> into sky

What is the price that must be paid by the person who learns to see and love the gorgon? He must 'drop his memory' of his former aesthetic, as America will learn, in Hughes's prophecy, to think beautiful what it formerly thought, under a more restricted aesthetic, repellent. And what will happen to Medusa once she is stellified? Her hair, once represented as serpentine, but in reality a liquid darkness with its 'cool suck' and 'shiver,' will become, in the astral cold, something like a halo of icicles: 'My hair/dry water.' Let me reproduce this mythological tale of the redemption of blackness once more:

> I've got to go
> down where my eye
> can't reach
> hairy star
> who forgets to shiver
> forgets the cool suck
> inside
>
> Someday long
> off someone will
> see me
> fling me up
> until I hook
> into sky
>
> drop his memory
>
> My hair
> dry water

This manner of dealing with blackness – non-autobiographical, mythological, cryptic – is a far cry from the journalistic demeanor of 'Stitches,' or, looking back, from the historical focus of the slave narratives, the geographical exoticism of 'Parsley' and 'Agosta,' and the realistic sequences of *Thomas and Beulah*. The severe geometry of form in 'Medusa' suggests the power of Dove's writing to embody a black identity without being constricted by it to a single manner. More than any other contemporary black poet, Dove has taken on the daunting aesthetic question of how to be faithful to, and yet unconstrained by, the presence – always already given in a black American – of blackness. She earns, by a poem like 'Medusa,' her epigraphs prefacing sections of *Grace Notes* – Cavafy's clear-eyed advice, 'Don't hope for things elsewhere' (*GN*,57), and Claude McKay's celebratory remark on 'the dark delight of being strange' (*GN*,45). When Whitman remarked, in the *Song of the Exposition*, that the Muse had left Greece, and had come to inhabit America – 'She's here, install'd amid the kitchen ware!' – he, alone among our nineteenth-century poets, might have foreseen that in one of her incarnations this American Muse would be one with the terrifying Medusa-face of slavery, but a Medusa who would become – by taking her liberty into her own hands, offering herself to a recognizing love, and making art out of the given of blackness – an American icon of the beautiful.

IV
JORIE GRAHAM:
THE NAMELESS AND
THE MATERIAL

———

Jorie Graham, the fourth of my instances of postwar American poetry, is what used to be called a philosophical poet. Her original *donnée* is a complex one, consisting, linguistically, of trilingualism in American English, Italian, and French. 'I was taught three//names for the tree facing my window..../ *Castagno*..../*Chassagne*..../And then *chestnut*.'¹ Graham grew up in Italy, though born of American parents – a Jewish-American artist mother and an Irish-American writer father. To borrow a phrase from Seamus Heaney, is it any wonder that when she thought she would have second thoughts? That second thought that we call philosophical wonder was reinforced in Graham by her schooling at the Rome Lycée Français, where, in philosophy class, students were regularly assigned essays on such intimidating abstractions as 'Justice' or 'Being.' Graham's family had close relations with other writers, artists, and filmmakers in Rome, and in fact Graham first came to live in the United States in her twenties, when, after studying at the Sorbonne, she arrived at New York University to study filmmaking with Martin Scorcese. During the marriage that gave her the name Graham, she studied writing at both Columbia University and the University of Iowa. She is now Professor of English in the Writer's Workshop at Iowa, where she and her husband, the poet and essayist James

Galvin, both teach. (Her daughter Emily appears occasionally in the poems.)

I mention these biographical facts because they help to explain some of the thematic features of Graham's writing – Italy (its landscapes, its saints), the history of the Holocaust (seen in recurring episodes), and the work of both early and modern painters (Piero della Francesca, Luca Signorelli, Klimt, Pollock, Rothko). They also help to account for certain technical aspects of her poetry – its cinematic strategies (close and far focus, panning, jump-cutting, emphasis on point of view and on looking), its recourse to enfolded European historical vignettes, its persistent use of philosophical diction, and, most centrally, its trying-on of several different linguistic expressions for the 'same thing' – as though language itself offered no perfect match for the material world, and as though 'English' were a congeries of sub-languages, each with its own 'flavor.' Most of all, I suspect, the rhythms of Italian – the language which surrounded Graham from her youngest years – lie behind her music in English. It was that music – a set of rhythms I hadn't heard before in American poetry – which first drew me to Graham, many years ago, when a few poems of hers were printed in *The American Poetry Review*.

Platonic dualism is both Graham's *donnée* and her demon; her recent names for the antagonists in that dualism – Matter and Interpretation – show the Protean variability of the terms of dualism under her hands.[2] She brings into postwar American poetry the urgent and inescapable need of the modern writer to embody in art a non-teleological universe – a universe without philosophical coherence though bound by physical law, a universe unconscious of us but which constitutes, by its materiality, our consciousness. For Graham, what used to be called spirituality is a fact of life as self-evident as materiality. Perhaps no-one brought up in Italy – with its

churches, its music, its paintings, its grandeur of aspiration –
could fail to think of the spiritual activity of consciousness as
wholly real and productive, something which deserves a
grander denomination than either of its secular names,
'thought' and 'aesthetic conception.' Graham's deepest subject
is how to represent the unboundedness and intensity of aspira-
tion as it extends itself to fullest self-reflexivity with ample
awareness of its own creative powers. But Graham refuses to
detach this metaphysical inquiry from either the passing per-
ceptual flow of the here-and-now or the hideous recollective
flow of the there-and-then that we call 'history.'

The tension caused in Graham's work by the counter-pulls
of aspiration, material perception, and historical accountability
assumes different forms in her five books, each substantially
longer than the one before: *Hybrids of Plants and of Ghosts*
(Princeton: Princeton University Press, 1980); *Erosion* (Princ-
eton: Princeton University Press, 1983); *The End of Beauty*
(New York: Ecco, 1987); *Region of Unlikeness* (New York: Ecco,
1991); and *Materialism* (Hopewell, N.J.: Ecco, 1993). These
books contain, by my count, 151 poems (some of them long
sequences) occupying some 500 pages. Like Lowell and Berry-
man, Graham has produced a daunting body of work, but
since it is only now beginning to receive critical codification,
there are in her case few received ideas to work with or
against. I will track Graham's journey from the unnameable
toward 'materialism' – a word in itself already problematic –
by considering one typical and thoroughly achieved poem
from each of her books, conscious of how limited a sample of
her work is thereby afforded, but firm in my belief that these
five poems are representative of her ambitious pursuit of a
new poetry, as 'material' as it is 'spiritual.'

Graham's first volume takes its arresting title from *Also
sprach Zarathustra*: 'But he who is wisest among you, he also is

only a discord and hybrid of plant and of ghost.'³ The animal, as a category, is conspicuously absent from this formulation. While plants are material, they are neither carnal nor appetitive; and ghosts, deprived of corporeality, have memory but not sensual perception. Human beings are discords, hybrids, then, but also curiously deprived (in this Nietzschean formulation) of immersion in the body. The body is a site of puzzlement, its relation to thought almost unformulatable. In *Hybrids of Plants and of Ghosts*, Graham's love of conceptual pattern – of the orienting grids of thought – questions, over and over, its perpetually vexed relation to sensory perception even before the two are formulated in language. Here is the poem 'The Geese,' which displays two contrasting patterns – one in the sky, made by the ambitious, goal-directed 'conceptual' paths of migrating geese, and another, parallel one on the earth, made by the textual netting of spiderwebs. There are two organizing remarks in the poem. The first remark expresses a fear of being overwhelmed by 'texture' – the infinite web-like registering of perceptual data that cannot be codified either by time (into 'history') or by space (into 'place'); the second remark expresses a dissatisfaction with the voyaging mind alone, since the body tells the mind that in its lofty activity it has missed something crucial, 'a bedrock poverty':

The Geese

Today as I hang out the wash I see them again, a code
as urgent as elegant,
tapering with goals.
For days they have been crossing. We live beneath these geese

as if beneath the passage of time, or a most perfect heading.
Sometimes I fear their relevance.
Closest at hand,
between the lines

the spiders imitate the paths the geese won't stray from,
imitate them endlessly to no avail:
things will not remain connected,
will not heal,

and the world thickens with texture instead of history,
texture instead of place.
Yet the small fear of the spiders
binds and binds

the pins to the lines, the lines to the eaves, to the pincushion bush,
as if, at any time, things could fall further apart
and nothing could help them
recover their meaning. And if these spiders had their way,

chainlink over the visible world,
would we be in or out? I turn to go back in.
There is a feeling the body gives the mind
of having missed something, a bedrock poverty, like falling

without the sense that you are passing through one world,
that you could reach another
anytime. Instead the real
is crossing you,

your body an arrival
you know is false but can't outrun. And somewhere in between
these geese forever entering and
these spiders turning back,

this astonishing delay, the everyday, takes place.

                    (*Hybrids*, 38–39)

The two patterns – the skyey adventurousness of the geese,
the anxious closures of the spiders – dictate the alternately
expansive and contracting lines of Graham's stanzas. Unable
to decide between the directed urgency of the mind and the
restrictive chainlink of perception, Graham stops 'somewhere

in between,' in 'the astonishing delay, the everyday.' (Later, in *The End of Beauty*, she will write a poem called 'Self-Portrait as Hurry and Delay,' where the spiders' weavings have turned into Penelope's web.)

'The Geese' is original in its juxtaposition of two matching and yet contrastive instinctual patterns, and in its refusing to choose one over the other, instead taking as its resting-place the 'delay' between them. Yet the stanzas in which these things take place are, perhaps, imperfectly articulated with the crux that stimulates them, the relation of body to mind. The two movements that close the poem – the one, a mental fall without a sense of traversing reality; the other, the real that 'cross[es] you' in a false 'arrival' in the body – are not quite clear enough in themselves or in their relation to the adventurous geese and the spiders fearfully binding things against a potential disintegration. And yet the perplexity they embody is at least partially conveyed: that all perception arrives first at and through the body, and that the ambitious mind cannot 'outrun' the body, which always precedes it. How to give bodily perception its due in thought is a question already vexing Graham's verse. How to match thought and perception with language remains as yet an unnamed problem.

The procedure of 'The Geese' is one that many of Graham's early poems will follow. First, a mundane beginning (here, 'hang[ing]out the wash') situates the speaker in the natural world; then, a natural emblem or set of emblems (here, the geese and spiders) is carefully rendered; next, a quasi-philo-sophical formulation of a problem is offered; and finally there appears a resolution, which may, and often does, evade the terms in which 'philosophy' has posed (or would pose) the original problem. The Wittgensteinian move away from the original anterior and imprisoning concepts (which would

[96]

always dictate a solution within their own terms) is a liberating one for Graham here as elsewhere – and is enacted, in 'The Geese,' by the single concluding line of the poem, with its 'astonishing delay, the everyday,' freeing the awaited remainder of its incomplete stanza into invisibility, openness and escape.

In 'The Geese,' 'history' is only a word. Graham's natural emblems, the geese and spiders, are themselves detached from history; and 'the everyday,' while it gives something in place of appalling random 'texture,' does not embody memory, either personal or historical, but remains an interval, without any apparent continuity with the past. Elsewhere in Graham's first volume, the past frightens by its destructive completeness – it is too great to be remembered, and too intimidating in its gaps representing the forgotten, 'the world too large to fit.' In the poem 'Framing' (*Hybrids*, 35), which puts, implicitly, the question of how closely representation matches reality, Graham sees herself, in a childhood photograph, looking at something the photo leaves out:

Something is left out, something left behind. As, for instance,

in this photo of myself at four, the eyes
focus elsewhere, the hand interrupted mid-air by some enormous sudden,
fascination.

What was the lost object of the child's arrested glance? One will never know, because it is not in the photo/memory:

Within, it would have been a mere event,
not destructive as it is now, destructive as the past remains,

becomes, by knowing more than we do.

We might have foreseen, given this poem, that Graham would have to go on to recover the destructive past – not only in her personal history but in some more general history of

[97]

human behavior, that which is 'outside' the personal snapshot. And by the time of *Erosion*, her next book, she is able to see that (to quote one poem called 'Mother of Vinegar') 'contained damage makes for beauty' (*Erosion*, 36). A fear of infinite extension like that ascribed in 'Geese' to the spiders generates the word 'contained' in this phrase, but the phrase expresses as well a hope for a new beauty that can incorporate the destructive past. Often, in *Erosion*, the past appears through past artists – Klimt, Keats, Herzog, Goya, Berryman, Masaccio, Signorelli. But there are other, more dangerous, appearances of the material past, such as the exhumed and blackened body of Saint Clare in Assisi, the spectacle of Graham's grandmother in the Jewish Geriatric Home on Long Island, or, most hazardously (in a poem called 'History'), events of World War II. (The title 'History' is one that Graham will re-use, twice, in *Region of Unlikeness*, a volume that also contains poems called 'Short History of the West' and 'The Phase after History').

I do not want to take the poem 'History' as my representative example from *Erosion*, because Graham will treat the theme of history more successfully later. But I do want to point out that this poem raises a topic that reappears in her recent volume *Materialism* – the denial, on the part of some skeptics (not to give them a worse name), of the reality of the Holocaust. In 'History,' Graham juxtaposes to a mention of that denial a 1942 photograph of a 'man with his own/genitalia in his mouth and hundreds of/slow holes/a pitchfork has opened/over his face,' as though documentary evidence could refute the skeptic's desire that the Holocaust be deniable. As if dissatisfied herself with the witness of bloodless photography, Graham offers a more potent emblem of history: sitting before an evening fire in the hearth, a man is blinded and his wife killed as a left-over grenade from the war, embedded in the tree the man has chopped up for firewood, explodes (*Erosion*,

[98]

64–65). History, then, is not a two-dimensional remnant, like a photograph; it is an active force, like the delayed violence of the grenade. And history does not simply record; it evaluates:

> For history
> is the opposite
> of the eye
> for whom, for instance, six million bodies in portions
> of hundreds and
> the flowerpots broken by a sudden wind stand as
> equivalent.
>
> (*Erosion*, 64)

The anger behind such a statement is as yet unmodulated by exploration of both recorded history and the (variously motivated) denial of history. When Graham returns, in *Materialism*, to Lyotard's supposition-for-argument's-sake that there can be no history of victimage because the victims, being absent, cannot testify to the event of their disappearance, she presents his discourse as one of many discourses competing for materialization in the world, all of them comprising the unavoidable dialectic in which the poet necessarily moves.

I return now from this anticipatory digression on Graham's first poem called 'History' to quote the more successful work I want to take as my representative example from *Erosion*: the poem called 'At Luca Signorelli's Resurrection of the Body.' This poem is written in the short, musing, in-and-out delaying phrases that characterize Graham's style at this period, phrases grouped in an orderly stanzaic style standing for gradual and patient advance, advance, advance – without any real promise of final closure. These phrases reflect, in this poem, Graham's sense of Signorelli's deliberate search for accuracy, as he dissected corpses so as to understand human musculature and articulation:

... In his studio
            Luca Signorelli
    in the name of God
            and Science
    and the believable
            broke into the body

studying arrival.
            But the wall
    of the flesh
            opens endlessly,
    its vanishing point so deep
            and receding

we have yet to find it,
            to have it
    stop us. So he cut
            deeper,
    graduating slowly
            from the symbolic

to the beautiful. How far
            is true?

It is because of his patient dissection that Signorelli can leave behind the flat, symbolic, medieval rendering of persons and depict instead, with unprecedented accuracy and intimacy, the actual beauty of flesh. This is nowhere more evident than in the great painting (from which Graham takes her poem) of the Resurrection of the Bodies in the Cappella Nuova of Orvieto Cathedral. The doctrine of the General Resurrection symbolizes, of course, the insufficiency of the soul alone as a representation for the human: though the redeemed dead enjoy eternal blessedness without their bodies, and presumably could do so forever, nonetheless, at the Last Judgment, when time comes to an end, the bodies of the dead will be reconstituted, and the souls in heaven will be allowed reunion with their long-lost flesh.[5]

Signorelli, with enormous sympathy for the prolonged yearning for the body which he imagines must be felt, even in heaven, by the disembodied souls of the dead, shows them on the Last Day eagerly re-finding their individual bodies – names, speech, perfected human flesh – and finding human company once again, too, in the re-animated bodies of others. Unable merely to rejoice in the moment with Signorelli and his subjects, the speaker in Graham's poem persistently questions the premise of the painting – that the eagerness of the spirit to rejoin the flesh is understandable and good:

> See how they hurry
>> to enter
> their bodies,
>> these spirits.
> Is it better, flesh,
>> that they
>
> should hurry so?
>> From above
> the green-winged angels
>> blare down
> trumpets and light. But
>> they don't care,
>
> they hurry to congregate,
>> they hurry
> into speech, until
>> it's a marketplace,
> it is humanity. But still
>> we wonder
>
> in the chancel
>> of the dark cathedral,

is it better, back?
    The artist
has tried to make it so: each tendon
    they press

to re-enter
    is perfect. But is it
perfection
    they're after,
pulling themselves up
    through the soil

into the weightedness, the color,
    into the eye
of the painter?

    . . .

    . . . They keep on
    arriving,
wanting names,
    wanting

happiness.

The speaker warns the heedless spirits that 'there is no en-
trance, / only entering.' The illimitable nature of sense-percep-
tion guarantees, for Graham, that one is never at rest in the
body; once one possesses a body, the clear geometric absolutes
of the spirit are confused by the ceaseless profusion of sense-
data that must somehow be put into relation with the knowl-
edge proper to the soul. This is an interminable process –
'there is no / entrance, / only entering.'

    It is only now that Graham can face the question that must
conclude Signorelli's progress from the Medieval symbolic to
the Renaissance beautiful: 'How far is true?' Modernity, be-
cause of the importance it ascribes to empirical knowledge,
demands that art be true as well as beautiful; and Signorelli,

pursuing his Renaissance aesthetic ideal of a believable and beautiful rendering of flesh, has almost unwittingly stumbled, through his dissections, on empiricism. And yet the word 'true' for Graham does not mean representational accuracy or scientific accuracy alone; the true, for an artist, must involve the accurate transmutation of feeling into knowledge, perception into categorization. Therefore, to close her poem, Graham invokes the exemplary anecdote of Luca Signorelli's dissection of the body of his son, dead by violence. Signorelli finds the true mending of grief in acquiring an exhaustive knowledge of the effects of violent death on the flesh of his flesh:

When his one son
    died violently,
he had the body brought to him
    and laid it

on the drawing-table,
    and stood
at a certain distance
    awaiting the best
possible light, the best depth
    of day,

then with beauty and care
    and technique
and judgement, cut into
    shadow, cut
into bone and sinew and every
    pocket

in which the cold light
    pooled.
It took him days
    that deep
caress, cutting,

unfastening,

until his mind
could climb into
the open flesh and
mend itself.

Like 'The Geese,' this poem ends with an incomplete stanza. The body of his son cannot appear to Signorelli under the sign of the symbolic or the sign of the beautiful; it bears the wound of truth, and the father's mind, wounded by the wound of the son, has further to go as the poem ends two-thirds of the way through a stanza. The extended analytic process of examining grief under a cold light is, for Graham as for Signorelli, the necessary precedent to art. Fact, including the fact of feeling, must undergo a long testing by analytic understanding before it can become, as art, 'true.' The body, in this formulation, becomes the subject of intimate and prolonged examination by the investigative mind; and it is in this somewhat uneasy way, with a 'mended' mind dominating the extinguished body, that Graham here reconciles the cohabitation of the spirit with the flesh. Even the violence of history can be contained within analysis; but the earlier aphorism, 'Contained damage makes for beauty,' has now to be emended to 'Damage, if investigated in a cold light, can be contained in beauty insofar as beauty is an ongoing entrance into the true.' Materialism, for Graham at this point, is still governed by intellectual analysis; and the true, even if it is a process rather than a conclusion, comes by even and measured and deliberate steps by the spirit through the evidence of matter. Yet against the closing image of Signorelli mending his marred heart by analysis of his son's body, we feel the earlier-described desire of the spirits of the dead, who want not to analyze the body but to join its living self in ecstatic oneness. That sensual desire, too, is Graham's own, and it is bound to come into conflict with the 'cold'

[104]

analytic desire of the mind. Which is the truth of 'materialism'
– its estatic livingness or its cold otherness?

The End of Beauty, Graham's third book, explores this ques-
tion most thoroughly in a poem too long to quote or to
unravel here, 'Pollock and Canvas' (81–89). Signorelli's ex-
ploratory dissection of the single contained physical unit will
not serve any longer as a metaphor for the relation of mind to
body, of the interpretative to the material. Jackson Pollock's
drip paintings contain too much of the improvisational and
the accidental in their aesthetic for any pre-ordained analytic
idea to govern their execution. Graham asks, here, whether
one can 'let . . . the made wade out into danger,/let . . . the
form slur out into flaw, in-//conclusiveness?' (86) If so, then
chance begins to play an increasingly large part in creation,
as even God discovered when his first creatures encountered
the serpent, changing the story as he had envisaged it:

> Then He rested letting in chance letting in
> any wind any shadow quick with minutes, and whimsy,
> through the light, letting the snake the turning
> in. Then things not yet true
> which slip in
>
> are true,
> aren't they?

Pollock's suspended stream of paint – as he bends over the
canvas painting vertically, not horizontally – is presided over
by one of the Graces, but not a conventionally aesthetic one:
she is 'this girl all accident all *instead-of*, of the graces the/
most violent one, the one all gash, all description.' By avoiding
the usual position of artist and easel, and by using drips rather
than brushstrokes, Pollock hopes to change the very nature of
painting; and yet, mysteriously, he ends up creating a painting
in some way continuous with the tradition. 'Oh but we wanted

to paint what is not beauty, how can one paint what is/not beauty . . .?' asks Graham.

To allow a primacy of the material over the spiritual, to admit into art the unexpected detour, the chance event, whimsy even, is to be forced to abandon the neat stanzas of a 'classical' poem like the one about Signorelli. It is to allow an equal role to the sensual, to make form mirror the unstoppable avalanche of sensations and the equal avalanche of units of verbal consciousness responding to those sensations. This is a dualism of sorts, but more confusing than the Platonic and Cartesian dualism with which Graham had begun. The new dualism creates the chief group of poems in *The End of Beauty*, seven dual self-portraits. Here are their titles:

Self-Portrait As the Gesture between Them
Self-Portrait As Both Parties
Orpheus and Eurydice
Self-Portrait as Apollo and Daphne
Self-Portrait as Hurry and Delay
Self-Portrait as Demeter and Persephone
Noli Me Tangere

These poems make up more than a quarter of *The End of Beauty*, and draw on some of the chief myths of the West. The first two are about Adam and Eve; the next four are about personages from classical myth ('Self-Portrait as Hurry and Delay' is about Penelope as weaver and unweaver); and the last – which, were it named in the same fashion as the others, would have to be called 'Self-Portrait as Jesus and Mary Magdalen' – is about the encounter directly after the Resurrection, enacting Mary's wish to close the gap between herself and Jesus, and his requiring, by his 'Noli me tangere,' that the gap remain inviolate. These are very rich poems, suggesting variously that there is always a 'gesture between' two points of opposition; that there is a way to be 'both parties' at the same time; and that one may find a way to create an alternating current, so to speak, between the weaving of life into the temporary closure of a shaped text, and the unweaving of that text into a less closed form. Many of these poems would repay analysis as representations of female identity, not least 'Self-Portrait as Demeter and Persephone,' where Graham, herself a daughter, finds herself also the mother of a daughter, and suggests that both rôles in the myth are open to her at once. But since my topic is the material and its increasing claims on Graham, thematically, formally, and linguistically, I leave the question of genre (self-portraiture), and the question of gender (identities available to women) aside, and take as my exemplary text from *The End of Beauty* a poem called 'To the Reader' (23–25).

This is neither the most successful nor the most moving of the poems in the book, but it is the most ominous. Briefly put, it is about one square yard of earth: a girl wants to 'catalogue and press onto the page *all she could find in it* / and name.' It is her project 'for Science Fair' (most American secondary schools run a Science Fair exhibiting the individual experiments of the students). The project of the poem is another version of Signorelli's analysis, hoping to find adequate language for the given, but there is no longer available for inspection a self-contained unit like a body. Instead, what is scrutinized is an arbitrarily chosen and equally arbitrarily delimited sample of the earth, the planet itself being by reason of its immensity beyond total analysis. The rule of this partial analysis is that everything found within the arbitrarily chosen square-yard sample must be included:

> She took the spade and drew the lines. Right through
> the weedbeds, lichen, moss, keeping the halves of things that landed
> *in*

by chance, new leaves, riffraff the wind blew in –

. . . .

her hole in the loam like a saying in the midst of the field of patience,
fattening the air above it with detail,
an embellishment on the April air,
the rendezvous of hands and earth –

(24)

This sounds, as an incorporation of materialism, promising
– an aesthetic of the earth, yes, but geometrically and scientific-
ally delimited; an aesthetic of the totality, yes, but of a single
indicative sample of it; an aesthetic of chance, yes, but one in
which chance becomes – in a Herbertian word – an 'embellish-
ment'; an aesthetic of the rendezvous of the spiritual and the
material, yes, but one in which the spiritual is represented by
the diligent, executive, and earth-stained hand rather than by
the pure eye of contemplation. Surely that which the hand
excavates can be named? It is a temptation, for the poet, to
leave it at that:

> Say we leave her there, squatting down, haunches up,
> pulling the weeds up with tweezers,
> pulling the thriving apart into the true,
> each seedpod each worm on the way down retrieved into a
> plastic bag (shall I compare thee), Say we
>
> leave her there, where else is there to go?

After all, have we not satisfied our craving for the material?
'We want it to stick to us,' says Graham, 'hands not full but
not clean.' Yet the potential inadequacy of language (each
retrieved item demanding its own simile in 'shall I compare
thee') lurks as a danger to the catalogue.

The apparent satisfaction of this solution is suddenly
undone by a new imagining. What if this solid, palpable,

[108]

diggable, mined-for-comparison material gave way under-
neath us, and the hole in the loam suddenly became a true
see-through-able hole, a vacancy, the unnameable? It is only
now that we notice, at the beginning of the poem, the extent
to which the square-yard-cataloguing of the material world
has been described as a defense: 'I swear to you,' says Graham,
'she wanted back into the shut, the slow,//a ground onto
which to say This is my actual life, Good Morning':

> onto which to say That girl on her knees who is me
> is still digging that square yard of land up
> to catalogue.

The trouble, Graham sees, is that material place – that one
square yard of earth – is always already under interpretation
– it might be the very place 'where the gods fought the giants
and monsters'; and it may not be representative or indicative,
'not a chosen place but a place/blundered into.' A true aes-
thetic of the material could not impose a Platonic rectangle or
even a Linnaean taxonomy on its subject matter. The material,
as a realm, is consequently 'a place which is a meadow with a
hole in it' – the hole the possibility of interminable and open-
ended interpretation, as my bracketed unfoldings suggest:

and some crawl through such a hole to the other place
>   [descending like Orpheus, through earth to its antithesis, the
>   underworld; or like Freud, who beneath material life found
>   the unconscious]
and some use it to count with and buy with
>   [making mathematical and commercial interpretations of
>   material substance]
and some hide in it and see Him go by
>   [investing matter with a Christian core].

But these potential responses to matter's vulnerability to inter-
pretation – even if they represent Graham's own past inclina-

tions – are not now available to her. In the past, it is true, she had been drawn to antithesis, to 'the other place,' in her investigation of duality; and she had, in her 'Science Fair' phase, been attracted to an almost geological sampling of materiality. She had even felt, like Mary Magdalen, the yearning to reassure herself of the risen Jesus's materiality. But her new foreboding suspicion is that interpretation is not achieved by dividing matter into antitheses, nor by inventorying matter through taxonomy, nor by transcending matter through visionary yearning. The desire for interpretation is simply a yawning vacancy, lethal to all hope of integrated summary in language. Look long enough at anything with the close-focus of interpretation and you kill not only yourself as receptor but also your object of vision – encountering, in the moment of its extinction, only a recursive version of yourself starting over:

and to some it is the hole on the back of the man running

through which what's coming towards him is coming into him,
    growing larger,

a hole in his chest through which the trees in the distance are seen
    growing larger shoving out sky shoving out storyline

until it's close it's all you can see this moment this hole in his back

in which now a girl with a weed and a notebook appears.

By the time that the Science-Fair hole in the loam becomes a hole in the chest and then in the back of a fleeing man unable to escape the overwhelming presence of the world invading him, 'surface' has become treacherous, 'a meadow with a hole in it.' Terra firma has turned into 'terra infidel' (a phrase from Stevens' 'Esthétique du Mal' which Graham adopts in the poem 'The Right to Life' in *Materialism*).

The formal consequences, for Graham's verse, of the insusceptibility of matter to dependable interpretation are several.

The most evident one here is of course the way in which the ending of the poem returns us, in circular fashion, to the beginning: the 'girl with a weed and a notebook' reappears and must re-begin her Sisyphean task of examining a square yard of matter. The denial of closure in this almost mechanical way is, however, not a truly 'open' ending; and Graham will eventually repudiate the notion of a perpetual re-beginning in the same place. One cannot fill up the bottomless and lethal hole with another square yard of earth and start over.

If the first formal consequence of interpretative instability is a lack of true closure, the second, visible throughout *The End of Beauty*, is Graham's avoidance of her former regular stanzas in favor of units of unpredictable length. Stanzas were themselves reassuring in their recurrent isometric symmetry; Graham must now disassemble them, ostentatiously separating single lines by successive Arabic numbers, as though each line were a free-standing item, a freeze-frame in a stop-and-start film. This is her technique in the first, and very beautiful, Genesis-poem of *The End of Beauty*, 'Self-Portrait as the Gesture between Them' (3–8), in which Eve's proffering of the apple to Adam – a gesture made iconic by centuries of painting – stands for the will-to-deviate-from-the-preordained-story, for the necessary appearance, in all creative impulse, of the stranger-serpent:

1

The gesture like a fruit torn from a limb, torn swiftly.

2

The whole bough bending then springing back as if from sudden
sight.

3

The rip in the fabric where the action begins, the opening of the
narrowpassage . . .

15

so that she had to turn and touch him to give it away

16

to have him pick it from her as the answer takes the question . . .

24

the balance like an apple held up into the sunlight

25

then taken down, the air changing by its passage, the feeling of being
    capable,

26

of being not quite right for the place, not quite the thing that's
    needed,

27

the feeling of being a digression not the link in the argument,
a new direction, an offshoot, the limb going on elsewhere. . . .

31

and loving that error, loving that filial form, that break from
    perfection

32

where the complex mechanism fails, where the stranger appears in
    the clearing,

33

out of nowhere and uncalled for, out of nowhere to share the day.

Even in this truncated quotation, Graham's revision of the
ordinary form of narration is startlingly visible. Formally speak-
ing, 'smooth,' uninterrupted, unproblematic narration can no
longer, for Graham, represent experience, which is forever
probing, tentative, anticipatory, and open-ended, truly repre-
sented only when the slow increments by which it happens
are mimicked in unmistakable linguistic patterns of hesitation

and inquiry and gradual realization. The open-ended 'day' at the end – who knows what the serpent who has appeared 'out of nowhere' will provoke next? – certifies that the inaugurating 'gesture between them' is one of many that will follow. The self-portrait here must be a provisional one – and is, as I have said, followed by many other similarly provisional self-portraits as *The End of Beauty* unfolds. Language incorporates ever-smaller increments of experience in each of its provisional gestures towards formulation; is any single one of these numbered gestures satisfactory, for the name of the moment? That is the inquiry implicitly imposed by the form.

Writing about herself in the third person (the girl with the notebook, Eve) is, in Graham, another formal consequence of matter's resistance to interpretation. The apparently unproblematic access to the self afforded by the traditional lyric 'I' suggests that there is only one conceivable self-portrait, not the successive ones afforded by, for instance, a triangulation of the self through myth – Graham's principal tactic in *The End of Beauty*. Another formal consequence of the freeze-frame representation of the spontaneous evolving of experience is Graham's reliance on the present participle as the principal grammatical vehicle of perception. Thus she suspends both the past (the principle of that which has been extinguished) and the future (the principle of that which will be extinguished), and writes in 'the delay' between the two. But the present participle cannot forever bar from Graham's sight either history (the past) or eschatology (the determined future). It is no accident that in Graham's next volume, *Region of Unlikeness*, history will struggle against presentness for domination. Though the present moment seems, in its perceptual fullness, nameable (if only just), the past, irretrievable and disputed, threatens to vanish utterly into the nameless.

The concerns about extinction of *Region of Unlikeness* are

presaged in the penultimate poem in *The End of Beauty*, an ode to the West Wind – 'stopless wind' – which derives from Shelley's ode, but which emphasizes throughout, unlike Shelley's ode, the purely abstract quality of the wind – 'wind of the theorems,/of proof, square root of light,//chaos of truth.' The 'endless evenness' of universal destruction, 'the race you start [the flowers] on and will not let them win,' is the law of extinction basic to the physical universe; and what can be the relation of this grim cosmic law to the law of human feeling and expression? 'What is your law to my law, unhurried hurrying?' asks Graham of the wind. Graham adapts her title for this poem, 'Of Forced Sightes and Trusty Ferefulness,' from Wyatt's Petrarchan sonnet, 'My galley charged with forgetfulness':

> My galley charged with forgetfulness
> Thorough sharp seas, in winter nights doth pass. . . .
> An endless wind doth tear the sail apace
> Of forced sighs, and trusty fearfulness. . . .
> Drowned is reason that should me confort,
> And I remain despairing of the port.

In homage to Wyatt's sonnet-quatrains, Graham writes her poem of the 'endless wind' in four-line stanzas, but stanzas of an irregularity that marks how far the modern verse of process must depart from the isometric quatrains of the sonnet tradition. By the end of the poem, as the poet attempts to join her law of song – drawn from the late autumn birds foraging for crumbs under her window – to the unstoppable destructive hurry of the cosmic wind, we can see that the old question from the Signorelli poem – 'How far is true?' no longer has the one-directional answer 'Further inside.' The trackless plain of the ocean is directionless, insusceptible to the rudder of analytic Reason:

> Oh hollow
> charged with forgetfulness
>
> through wind, through winter nights, we'll pass,
> steering with crumbs, with words,
> making of every hour
> a thought, remembering
>
> by pain and rhyme and arabesques of foraging
> the formula for theft
> under your sky that keeps
> sliding away
>
> married to hurry
> and grim song.

The 'white jury' of the wind turns away once its extinctions are completed, its 'deep justice done.' To investigate the justice of material extinction, perceptual and even metaphorical search will not suffice; evidence from history becomes necessary to the poet. Sensory presentness must give way, analytically, to 'the morning after.' The frustration of taking the long historical view, compared to the intimate close-focus view of present-participial writing, is expressed in a quasi-sonnet entitled 'Act III, Sc. 2' (66), its title suggesting that we are already half-way through the play:

> Look she said this is not the distance
> we wanted to stay at – We wanted to get
> close, very close. But what
> is the way in again? And is it
>
> too late? She could hear the actions
> rushing past – but they are on
> another track. And in the silence,
> or whatever it is that follows,
>
> there was still the buzzing: motes, spores,

aftereffects and whatnot recalled the morning after.
Then the thickness you can't get past called *waiting*.

Then the you, whoever you are, peering down to see if it's done yet.
Then just the look on things of being looked-at.
Then just the look on things of being seen.

This remarkable little poem represents an anthropomorphized Whitmanian God ('you, whoever you are' from 'As I Ebb'd with the Ocean of Life') who peers down at his creation to see if it is done yet, like a dish set to cook in an oven. At completion, it will be looked-at. After completion, it will be seen. History is something peered at by its composing author-deity, looked at when 'done' by its author-as-judge, and finally seen only by inhabitants of the next succeeding epoch. History, untranscendent, brings out in Graham the colloquial diction that mentions 'aftereffects and whatnot recalled the morning after.' History is a this-worldly thing, experienced by others precisely like ourselves, and therefore able to be discussed, at least in part, in terms that do not rise above the quotidian. Graham's tendency, in her first books, toward the exalted and the prophetic has been severely tempered, by the time she writes *Region of Unlikeness*, toward the material and the actual. Nonetheless, she remains determined not to let go of a principle of transcendent judgment, even in the presence of the unreliable and deniable chronicle we call history.

It is impossible that my exemplary poem from *Region of Unlikeness* should not be a poem called 'History' (the second of two so entitled in the volume). 'History' (89–93) is perhaps less formally inventive a poem than some others, those which begin to incorporate into Graham's previous resources (natural image and inner meditation) complex historical anecdotes of lived life – the attempted suicide of a student in 'The Phase after History'; the confinement of Graham's grandmother in a nursing home and the last moments of a young concentration-camp inmate in 'From the New World'. 'History' is important because it establishes the relation between the self and the necessitarian stopless wind of physical law – but the wind is now altered into the endless self-extension of history as a tethered beast chewing out the narratives that define it. The self, which seemed so fragile and unimportant under the cosmic wind, finds to its joy in 'History' that it is after all indispensable, and its indispensability resides in its capacity to define and register not only its own fate, but that of the world. This finding is dependent upon Graham's use of the Christian theological concept of *kairos* – the absolute moment of time at which it is necessary that something come to pass.

'History' presents, as it progresses, three foci. The first is a huge cloud of cacophonous black storks settling out of the sky and covering Graham's field of vision. These are messengers (versions of Graham's recurrent neutral angel of annunciation who heralds a new phase): 'This is newness? This is the messenger? Screeching. / Clucking.' The black storks unwrap the previously coherent fabric of the universe; and their dark settling, 'tripling the shadowload,' suggests the endless undoing of story by new story from Homer on:

> Look up and something's unwrapping –
> Look up and it's suitors, applause,
> it's fast-forward into the labyrinth.

The second focus of 'History' is a frozen river, concealing underneath its black ice-cover the beautiful transparency that used to reflect the human world. Her past, says the poet, is cast down with the rest of human history under that lid of ice:

Under the frozen river the other river flows
on its side in the dark
   now that it cannot take into itself
the faces, the eyes – the gleam in them – the tossed-up hand
   pointing then casting the pebble in.

Forget what we used to be, doubled, in the dark
age where half of us is cast
   in and down, all the way,
into the silt,
   roiled under,

saved in there with all the other slaughtered bits,
   dark thick fabric of the underneath,
sinking, sifting.

The third focus of the poem, after the storks and the river, is
Graham's surreal vision of history as an allegorical beast:
'Some part of it bleats, some part of it is/the front, has a
face.'[6] The chained beast, history, gnaws audibly on its narra-
tive bone, and the author wonders how she, or anyone, can
be a part, a significant part, of that train of events we call
'history':

Listen:
the x gnaws, making stories like small smacking

sounds,
   whole long stories which are its gentle gnawing. . . .
   If the x is on a chain, licking its bone,

making the sounds now of monks
   copying the texts out,
muttering to themselves,
   if it is on a chain
(the lights snapping on now all along the river)
   if it is on a chain

[118]

that hisses as it moves with the moving x,
   link by link with the turning x
(the gnawing now Europe burning)
   (the delicate chewing where the atom splits),
if it is on a chain –
   even this beast – seven this the favorite beast –
then this is the chain, the gleaming

   chain: that what I wanted was to have looked up at the right
time.

This unexpected description of history – with its gnawing
being at one moment monks in a scriptorium, at another war
in Europe, at still another atomic fission – reels out the past
while keeping it in the participial present: the author feels the
compulsion of the past without being able to let it be preterite,
and feels the compulsion of the present without being able to
let it be transient. This quandary is resolved by the notion of
kairos: 'that what I wanted [imperfect] was to have looked up
[perfect infinitive] at the right time' – a moment in history
strictly limited, without the luxurious spread of the participial
present, but also without the indifferent successivity of the
past. As the poet herself (through her use of the past tense and
the past indicative) becomes an element in a vanished history,
she also sees a historical function for herself; she will have had
significance if she succeeds in seeing and registering what she
was bred to see, what nobody but herself could have seen:

then this is the chain, the gleaming

   chain: that what I wanted was to have looked up at the right
time,
    to see what I was meant to see,
to be pried up out of my immortal soul,
   up, into the sizzling quick –

That what I wanted was to have looked up at the only
    right time, the intended time,
punctual,
    the millisecond I was bred to look up into, click, no
half-tone, no orchard of
    possibilities,

up into the eyes of my own
    fate not the world's.

This prayer – to have confronted one's own fate at the intended time, and thereby to have made visible to others, through language, a moment of history – must remain for every artist a prayer and a hope, rather than a certainty. The artist must return to the enigmatic present of experience; and 'History' ends with the black storks, 'shadows of shadows,' settling on the nearby tree, where 'The bough still shakes.'

In returning to its first visual focus, its storks, 'History' resembles 'To the Reader,' which returned at its close to its girl with her weed and her notebook, her perpetual task of description. But 'History' has replaced a diligent voluntary task with an expectant vigil for the fated vision; the task of the artist is not patient digging in the earth, but remaining ready to look up at just the right millisecond. The material – history – is always around us in the world, but something more electric than exhaustive investigation now marks the relation of interpretation to matter; poetic interpretation has an element of the prophetic and the fated and the visionary about it. By speaking from beyond the tomb – 'What I wanted was to have looked up at the only right time' – the speaker liberates herself both from her participially continued past and her immobilism in the present, and can place herself into a new relation with matter as it is incarnated as historical event. Language about history is as contingent as the 'beast' and its linked stories, but if uttered at the 'right' time will partake, however socially and historically constructed, of the shape of that historical moment.

The 'posthumous' self-placement of 'History' generates questions about 'the phase after history' – a phrase used as the title of a poem in *Region of Unlikeness*, a poem which appropriates the Macbeths' murder of Duncan, and their failure to form another viable dynasty, in order to question how one is to know the right millisecond one was born to look up into. Macbeth, deceived into thinking he had to grasp a particular moment, is a figure for the wrong interpretation of one's own fate, and therefore of the fate of the world. As Lady Macbeth relives in her sleepwalking the crucial failure of their moment, she cannot see an alternative action or a future redress. The poem 'The Phase after History' ends in consternation and bewilderment:

> Where is America here from the landing, my face on
>
> my knees, eyes closed to hear
> further?
> Lady M. is the intermediary phase.
> God help us.
> Unsexed unmanned.
> Her open hand like a verb slowly descending onto
> the free,
> her open hand fluttering all round her face now,
> trying to still her gaze, to snag it on
>
> those white hands waving and diving
> in the water that is not there.

(Region of Unlikeness, 120–21)

Trying to find a personal 'phase after history' is futile; and the last poem in *Region of Unlikeness*, following 'The Phase after History,' is spoken by the soul, relinquishing, like Prospero, her creative power in favor of her visible relic, song, which itself, having entered the universe, becomes a form of matter:

(This is a form of matter of matter she sang)

(Where the hurry is stopped) (and held) (but not extinguished) (no)

(So listen, listen, this will soothe you) (if that is what you want)

Now then, I said, I go to meet that which I liken to
(even though the wave break and drown me in laughter)
the wave breaking, the wave drowning me in laughter –
(*Region of Unlikeness*, 125)[7]

The impersonal gaiety of language replaces the drowning wave of death, and it turns out that no personal 'phase after history' is required. *Region of Unlikeness* closes as song, present in the world after the death of its maker, becomes a form of matter. By closing with the past tense words 'I said' ('Now then, I said, I go ...'), yet with that past tense enclosing a quotation inscribing the participial instant of drowning, Graham avoids both the posthumous gaze of 'What I wanted was to have looked up' and the repetitive and futile gestures of Lady Macbeth after her failed moment of historical agency.

And now Graham has called her most recent collection by a title we might have anticipated: *Materialism*. It is far too soon for any of us to have assimilated all these new poems into our knowledge of Graham, but not too soon for me to close with one of them. First, though, I want to say a word about the format of *Materialism*. It contains twenty-three poems; and interspersed among the poems are long excerpts, mostly in prose, from significant authors of the Western tradition, ranging from Francis Bacon to Walter Benjamin, from Plato to Wittgenstein, from Leonardo da Vinci to Walt Whitman, from Jonathan Edwards to Brecht. All of these excerpts treat in some way the materiality of the world and the materiality of language, and Graham has included them, presumably, to trace the long effort of the Western world to come to terms with the fact of matter. Perhaps the most unexpected prose excerpt is an uncanonical one from *McGuffey's New Fifth Reader*, in which the materiality of language is minutely examined – sometimes for purposes of class distinction, sometimes for simple taxonomical ends, sometimes for rote questioning, but never for the purpose of aesthetic discrimination:

> Is he sick, or is he well
> Is he young, or is he old
> Is he rich, or is he poor. . . .
>
> Do not say *chile* for child; *feller* for fellow;
> *fuss* for first; *kinely* for kindly. . . .
>
> (Where is the rising inflection marked? What is the rule?)
> (*Materialism*, 105–106)

The excerpts from Bacon's *Novum Organum*, on the other hand, show the new Renaissance moment of materialism exhibiting itself in a quasi-scholastic concentration on high–order discriminations among physical motions:

> Let the first motion be that of the resistance of matter. . . . Let the second motion be that which we term the motion of connection. . . . Let the third be that which we term the motion of liberty. . . . Let the fourth be that which we term the motion of matter. . . . Let the fifth be that which we term the motion of continuity. . . . Let the fourteenth motion be that of configuration or position. . . . Let the fifteenth motion be that of transmission or of passage. . . . Let the sixteenth be that which we term the royal or political motion. . . . Let the eighteenth motion be that of trepidation. . . . (*Materialism*)

In such a passage we see the fine distinctions of medieval theological discourse brought over, almost without change, into the realm of matter. Against such scientific examinations of matter, Graham sets Whitman's hymn (from 'Crossing Brooklyn Ferry') to material phenomena:

Appearances, now or henceforth, indicate what you are:

Thrive, cities! bright your freight, being your shows, ample and
        sufficient rivers:
Expand, being: keep your places objects.

We descend upon you and all things – we arrest you all:
We *realize* the soul only by you, you faithful solids and fluids: . . .

You have waited, you always wait, you dumb, beautiful
        ministers! . . .
We use you, and do not cast you aside – we plant you permanently
        within us:
We fathom you not – we love you.
        (*Materialism*, xi)

By setting her own poems among other forms of discourse on the material world (even assembling one lyric which defines the self by haiku appropriated from Shiki, Issa, Buson, and Kyorai), Graham, like Wordsworth, asserts that all discourse, Western and Eastern, including poetry, exists as one of the forms of matter found waiting for us in the universe, and is as 'real' as other phenomena. Poems cannot, then, be sequestered as a form of the transcendent or the immaterial. Nonetheless, it is not easy to bring matter and thought together in the form of poetry. Twice in *Materialism* Graham poses her central question, adapting it to the poem at hand:

(how can the water rise up out of its grave of matter?) –
  (how can the light drop down out of its grave of thought?) –
        ('Event Horizon,' 53)

How can the scream rise up out of its grave of matter?
How can the light drop down out of its grave of thought?
        ('Manifest Destiny,' 100)

[124]

If, in Graham's present view, the only reality the self can find is a reality defined by primary material phenomena, the poet can no longer compose self-portraits through mythological personae, as Graham did in the dual portraits in *The End of Beauty*. The self must now portray itself *in* primary matter; and there are five poems in *Materialism* called 'Notes on the Reality of Self,' as though a conviction of the reality of the self could only be arrived at afresh through a new set of material phenomenal equivalents. Yet the indifference of the material universe to our fate makes us hesitate to appropriate its phenomena as adequate symbols of ourselves. Graham re-examines the adequacy of the pathetic fallacy in the third of her 'Notes on the Reality of the Self' (10–11), which I will take as my exemplary poem from *Materialism*. In this and the other 'Notes,' Graham wishes to be fully faithful to the representation of phenomena, and to their ordinary material configurations, even as, through them, she defines the reality of the lyric self. As in the past, she chooses, in the third 'Notes,' several foci of attention. Here, the four foci are: first, the late afternoon light; second, the autumn wind (which we recall from 'Of Forced Sightes'); third, the reddish bushes in the speaker's yard which are agitated by, yet which also momentarily tame, that wind, and which are illuminated by that light; and fourth, the band which is practicing – with drums, trumpets, trombones, and French horns – in the nearby field.

The first configuration of the poem puts light, bushes, wind, and drumbeats together easily, unproblematically, as they all meet in the perceiving self of the speaker:

In my bushes facing the bandpractice field,
in the last light, surrounded by drumbeats, drumrolls,
there is a wind that tips the reddish leaves
exactly all one way, seizing them up from underneath, making them

barbarous in unison. Meanwhile the light insists they glow
where the wind churns.

Such a stable configuration is soon disturbed, and the light is
re-imagined as a ladder of gold in the sky, in and out of which the
limbs of the bushes roil. But language, always conscious of its
own arbitrariness and insufficiency, begins its drawing of distinc-
tions, and Graham asks, Is it the limbs – or the racks of limbs – or
the luminosities of branchings – that roil? and do they do it
always, or would a counter-description, one of stasis, be equally
true at a different moment, the moment when the wind drops?

> Meanwhile the light insists they glow
> where the wind churns, or, no, there is a wide gold corridor
> of thick insistent light, layered with golds, as if runged,
> as if laid low from the edge of the sky,
> in and out of which the coupling and uncoupling
> limbs – the racks of limbs – the luminosities of branchings –
> offspring and more offspring – roil – (except when a sudden
>   stillness reveals
> an appal of pure form, pure light –
> every rim clear, every leaf serrated, tongued – stripped
> of the gauzy quicknesses which seemed its flesh) –

It is no surprise that this brilliant passage, in its turn, requires
correction: 'but then the instabilities/regroup.' The purely
visual scene so far described is now yet further complicated by
the full acoustic entrance of the drumroll and brassy music
from the nearby field.

Up to this point, the poem seems not to justify its title –
'Notes on the Reality of the Self.' Where is the self in these
struggles towards configuration made by light, wind, bushes,
and drums? It is only in the second half of the poem, which
turns from narration to question, that the darker underside of

perception appears. The speaker, it is true, can easily encom-
pass within herself light, wind, bushes, and drums: it is even
true that as they change she can change kinesthetically with
them. But if one removes lyric subjectivity, and thinks purely
about these four material foci of the poem, impenetrability at
once becomes the central problem. The bushes, to put it simply,
cannot hear the drumbeats and the trumpets. The bushes can
bend to the wind, it is true; but they do not bend to sonic
waves. If one imagines human beings as matter, then one is
struck by despair at one's own limitations; there are spectra
one cannot see, there are sounds one cannot hear. We must
be in some way very like those bushes, which are impermeable
to the torrent of sound pouring around them: and we are also
like the drumbeats, forever beating in vain at an unhearing
material world. In the despair of the mutually uncomprehend-
ing bushes and drumbeats, we see the despair of the self as
matter, with its perceptual receptivity so far from being infi-
nite, its expressivity in language so far from being universally
receivable:

Tell me, where are the drumbeats which fully load and expand
each second,
bloating it up, cell-like, making it real, where are they
to go, what will *they* fill up
pouring forth, pouring round the subaqueous magenta bushes
which dagger the wind back down on itself,
tenderly, prudently, almost loaded down˙
with regret? For there is not a sound the bushes will take
from the multitude beyond them, in the field, uniformed –
(all left now on one heel) (right) (all fifty trumpets up
to the sun) – not a molecule of sound
from the tactics of this glistening beast,
forelimbs of silver (trombones, french horns)

(anointed by the day itself) expanding, retracting,
bits of red from the surrounding foliage deep
        in all the fulgid
instruments – orient – ablaze where the sound is released
trumpeting, unfolding –
               screeching, rolling, patterning, measuring –
scintillant beast the bushes do not know exists.

To this blazing explosion of the monstrous collective band –
splendidly imagined and rendered – the bushes are forever
deaf and blind. This is a damning admission for the perceptual
self, itself matter-as-bush, to make; and a disheartening admis-
sion for the expressive self, itself matter-as-collective-music, to
acquiesce in.

The bushes are not only deaf and blind, they are powerless.
As we last see them, the light has gone and they are left in the
power of 'a wind that does not really even now exist,'

      in which these knobby reddish limbs that do not sway
              by so much as an inch
    its arctic course
          themselves now sway –

By submitting herself as chameleon-identity to bush and drum-
roll, themselves acted on by wind and light (those almost
immaterial things), Graham has explored not only the limita-
tions of any conceivable material self, but also the poetic
expression possible to a self conceiving itself as matter. Al-
though such a self can begin equably enough in sense-percep-
tion, it cannot assert the sort of mastery over experience that
the teleological self was wont to display – choosing to stay the
fair moment for inspection, admitting no other petitioner to its
attention. The instabilities of matter must now be assumed by
the self; and so any poem spoken in the voice of the material

self must be an unstable poem, constantly engaged in linguistic processes of approximation. The material self is limited, and must enact that limitation (here, through two different material personae, the bushes and the band). And the material self is ultimately powerless over fate, and cannot wrench fate to a satisfying eschatological closure: the unswayable arctic wind, the swaying bushes, engage in a stand-off with each other, with fate the ultimate master.

The real power latent in the idea of the poetic self conceived as matter emerges in Graham's intense and lavish transcriptions of the material world, in which all her formidable energies of description and kinesis are engaged. Graham's attempt to describe the material world with only minimal resort to the usual conceptual and philosophical resources of lyric (once so dear to her), and to make that description a vehicle for her personal struggle into comprehension and expression, is harder even than it would seem. In *Materialism*, Graham is willing to blend all her abundant talent to the description of something as evanescent as a beam of sun infiltrating a room and passing over a spectator ('Subjectivity', part 2, 26–29), or to the gradual opening of an amaryllis bud ('Opulence,' 134–35). There is a great deal more that could be said about this recent book, with its valiant resolve to remain, linguistically speaking, on the material plane. It bravely closes with the old classical pun on vegetal leaves and the leaves of a book; Graham's leaves are carried on the surface by the current of the river, carried away in time even from their mortal author:

> The river still ribboning, twisting up,
>   into its re-
> arrangements, chill enlightenments, tight–knotted
>   quickenings

and loosenings – whispered messages dissolving
　　　　　　　the messengers –
the river still glinting-up into its handfuls, heapings,
　　　　　　　　　　glassy
forgettings under the river of
my attention – . . .
and the surface rippling over the wind's attention –
rippling over the accumulations, the slowed-down drifting
　　　　　　　　　　　permanences
of the cold
bed.
I say *iridescent* and I look down.
The leaves very still as they are carried.
　　　　　　('The Surface,' 143)

In these knottings and loosenings, slowings and quicken-
ings, ending in, stopping on, a word, Graham finds the only
linguistic and imaginative equivalents for the self as she now
understands it. Because the phenomena of perception are for
the trilingual poet detached from any one language of embodi-
ment, they exist finally as metaphysical notions, transiently
embodied but never finally capturable in form. It is odd, but
logical, that a given so generous as three available languages
should result, as it does, in a made art more diaphanous, more
restless, and more metaphysical than any other contemporary
American poetic construct.

NOTES

Notes

British and American publication details of volumes from which extracts are quoted in these Notes; page references are to the American editions (whose contents and pagination sometimes differ from the British editions).

Introduction

1 Ian Hamilton, *Robert Lowell* (New York: Random House, 1982; London: Faber and Faber, 1983), 337–38. Biographical facts about Lowell and quotations from his letters are drawn from this biography.

2 Robert Lowell, *History* (New York: Farrar, Straus & Giroux; London: Faber and Faber, 1973), 140.

I

1 John Thompson, 'Robert Lowell, 1917–1977,' in Jeffrey Myers, ed., *Robert Lowell: Interviews and Memoirs* (Ann Arbor: University of Michigan Press, 1988), 237.

2 *Complete Poems*, ed. Francis X. Murphy (New York and London: Penguin, 1986), 611.

3 *Ibid.*, 41.

4 Robert Lowell, *Collected Prose*, ed. Robert Giroux (New York: Noonday, 1987; London: Faber and Faber, 1989), 255.

5 Hamilton, 76.
6 *Ibid.*, 85.
7 *Ibid.*, 99.
8 Robert Lowell, *Selected Poems* (New York: Noonday, 1977), 25. Henceforth, quoted poems from the *Selected Poems* will be followed by page numbers referring to this volume.
9 Robert Lowell, *Lord Weary's Castle and The Mills of the Kavanaughs* (New York: Farrar, Straus & Giroux, 1974), 88.
10 Hamilton, 180.
11 *Ibid.*, 196.
12 *Ibid.*, 201.
13 *Ibid.*, 221.
14 *Ibid.*, 222.
15 *Ibid.*, 223.
16 'After Enjoying Six or Seven Essays On Me,' *Salmgundi*, 37 (Spring 1977), 112–115.
17 Lowell, *Prose*, 221.
18 Hamilton, 234.
19 *Ibid.*, 237.
20 *Ibid.*, 258.
21 *Ibid.*, 272.
22 Ferris Greenslet, *The Lowells and Their Seven Worlds* (London: Ernest Benn, 1947), 252.
23 Hamilton, 301.
24 *Ibid.*, 307.
25 'Et in America Ego,' *Listener*, 82, 4 September 1969, 302–304, rpt. Jeffrey Myers, 141–42.
26 *Ibid.*, 142.
27 Dudley Young, 'Talk with Robert Lowell,' *New York Review of Books*, 4 April 1971, 32–33, rpt. Myers, 148–153, 152.
28 Robert Lowell, *Notebook 1967–68* (New York: Farrar, Straus & Giroux, 1969; London: Faber and Faber, 1970), 160. Future quotations from this volume will be identified parenthetically in the text, preceded by the abbreviation N.
29 Lowell, *Prose* (252).

30 Lowell, *Day by Day* (New York: Farrar, Straus & Giroux, 1977; London: Faber and Faber, 1978). Future quotation will be parenthetically identified preceded by the abbreviation *D*.

II

1 I wish to thank Alan Lathrop, Curator of the Manuscripts Division of the University of Minnesota Libraries, and his Assistant, Barbara Bezat, for their kind assistance in my use of the Berryman papers. I am most grateful to Kathleen Donohue (Mrs John Berryman) for permission to reprint unpublished material from the Berryman papers.

2 *Notebook 1967–68* (New York: Farrar, Straus & Giroux, 1969; London: Faber and Faber, 1970), 151.

3 Robert Lowell, *Day by Day* (New York: Farrar, Straus & Giroux, 1977; London: Faber and Faber, 1978), 27–28.

4 John Berryman, *Collected Poems 1937–1971*, ed. Charles Thornbury (New York: Farrar, Straus & Giroux, 1989; London: Faber and Faber, 1970), xxxvii.

5 *Ibid.*, 70.

6 *Ibid.*, 55.

7 John Berryman, *The Dream Songs* (New York: Farrar, Straus & Giroux, 1969; London: Faber and Faber 1990), vi. Henceforth abbreviated *DS* in parenthetical citations.

8 John Berryman, unpublished note to *The Dream Songs*, in John Haffenden, *John Berryman: A Critical Commentary* (New York: New York University Press, 1980), 59. Every writer on Berryman must be grateful, as I am, for this commentary and for Haffenden's *Life of John Berryman* (Boston: Routledge & Kegan Paul, 1982), the two books which first brought Berryman's life and unpublished manuscripts into public scrutiny.

9 John Berryman, *The Freedom of the Poet* (New York: Farrar, Straus & Giroux, 1976), 316.

10 *Commentary*, 83–84.

11 Berryman papers, University of Minnesota, loose sheet, undated

but written after Berryman's arrival in Minneapolis, as can be seen from an itinerary in the poem.

12 *Life*, 264, 306.

13 *Ibid.*, 375–76.

14 *Ibid.*, 351–52.

15 *Poems*, 79.

16 *Ibid.*, 107.

17 Berryman papers, University of Minnesota; see note 11.

18 Berryman spent months in 1954 analyzing his dreams, writing them down at tedious length as the dreams of 'St. Pancras Braser,' in a manuscript now preserved in the Berryman papers at the University of Minnesota.

19 *Poems*, 41.

20 *Ibid.*, 22.

21 *The Freedom of the Poet*, 303.

22 *Poems*, xxxv.

23 Avila notebook, Berryman papers, University of Minnesota, 3.

24 Notebook of 2 November 1959, Berryman papers, University of Minnesota.

25 *The Sickness unto Death* by S. Kierkegaard, tr. Walter Lowrie (Princeton, 1941), much marked, and signed 'J.B., Princeton 30 October 1943' is now kept in the Wilson Library of the University of Minnesota.

26 *Ibid.*, 83.

27 *Ibid.*, 86.

28 *Ibid.*, 106–107.

III

1 Quotations parenthetically identified in the text are cited from Rita Dove, *Selected Poems* (New York: Vintage, 1990, rpt. Pantheon, 1993).

2 *The First Suite* (from a novel in progress), in *Black American Literature Forum*, 20 (Fall 1986), 244. The passage, somewhat cut, appears in Dove's novel, *Through the Ivory Gate* (New York: Pan-

theon, 1992). What is cut out is the imagination: the extrapolated cone, the obsessive relation to the digital numbers, and the fantasy of the Babylonian merchant. These would all be entirely at home in a poem by Dove; her cutting them out of her novel suggests that she has not yet come, in her fiction, to a desirable integration of her imaginative with her tale-telling narrative impulses.

3 *Ibid.*, 245.

4 Here and elsewhere the correct date of the Haitian massacres, 1937, is mistranscribed as 1957. The event is described by Robert D. Crassweller, in his biography *Trujillo* (New York: Macmillan, 1966), 154–56, as follows:

> The terrible events of the thirty-six hours that began on the night of October 2 ... had surely been planned well in advance, as a kind of military operation. . . .
>
> In Santiago alone the [Dominican] Army rounded up between one and two thousand Haitians, herded them into a courtyard formed by government buildings, and systematically decapitated them with machetes, this weapon being used whenever possible in preference to firearms in order to simulate a spontaneous attack by an enraged Dominican peasantry. In Monte Cristi another large group of Haitians was marched at gunpoint to the end of the harbor pier, with arms bound, and simply pushed into deep water to drown. . . .
>
> A crude test was adopted to probe the claim of Dominican nationality which the terrified Haitians often cried out. Everyone was asked to say the Spanish word *perejil*, and those who pronounced it 'pelegil' were damned as Haitians and cut down without further ado. . . .
>
> The number of those who perished in these October hours will never be known with accuracy. . . . Estimates range from a low of 5,000 to a high of 25,000. The Haitian Government at one time put forth a figure of 12,000 fatalities, and Trujillo in later days spoke of 18,000. A figure between 15,000 and 20,000 would be a reasonable estimate, but this is guesswork. . . . An almost incredible time elapsed between the killings and the world's knowledge of them. The first public mention appeared in *The New York Times* on October 21, seventeen days after the events. . . . It reported rumors of a border clash in which 'several Haitians' had been shot.

Crassweller does not give a specific source for the story about the test-by-pronunciation. Jesús de Galíndez, in *The Era of Trujillo* –

published only in 1973 by the University of Arizona Press, Tucson, but submitted as a doctoral dissertation at Columbia University in 1956, shortly before Galíndez disappeared, probably kidnapped and murdered by Trujillo forces – does not mention the test; he does say that 'private sources mention 20,000 and even 25,000' killed (209).

5 'Conversation with Rita Dove,' ed. Stan Sanvel Rubin and Earl G. Ingersoll, *Black American Literature Forum*, 20 (Fall 1986), 230–31.

6 *Ibid.*, 230.

7 *Grace Notes* (New York and London: W. W. Norton, 1989), 31. Henceforth parenthetically cited as *GN*.

8 Langston Hughes, *Selected Poems* (New York: Vintage, 1990), 275.

IV

1 'I Was Taught Three,' in *Hybrids of Plants and of Ghosts* (Princeton: Princeton University Press, 1980), 4.

2 'Who Watches from the Dark Porch' in *Region of Unlikeness* (New York: Ecco Press, 1991), 97.

3 Dedicatory page, unnumbered.

4 'Annunciation with a Bullet in It,' (*Erosion*, 72). Graham's endnote, giving the reference to Lyotard's *Le Différand*, is on 146.

5 Graham's imagination will dwell once again on the Last Judgment (in Michelangelo's version) in the poem 'Chaos' (*Region of Unlikeness*, 46–53); there, the emphasis is on judgment rather than on the rejoining of soul and body.

6 This description may unconsciously owe something to the beast 'sophistication' described (in a quotation from the Greek Anthology) in Marianne Moore's poem, 'In the Days of Prismatic Color':

> 'Part of it was crawling, part of it
> was about to crawl, the rest
> was torpid in its lair.'
> (Marianne Moore, *Complete Poems* (New York: Macmillan, 1981; London: Faber and Faber, 1984), 41.)

[138]

7 The end of 'Soul Says' also contains an unconscious reminiscence,
I believe, of the end of Moore's 'In the Days of Prismatic Color':

> Truth is no Apollo
> Belvedere, no formal thing. The wave may go over it if it likes.
> Know that it will be there when it says,
>   'I shall be there when the wave has gone by.'
>
>   (Moore, *Complete Poems*, 42)